First and Second
Peter and Jude

Westminster Bible Companion

Series Editors

Patrick D. Miller
David L. Bartlett

First and Second Peter and Jude

FRED B. CRADDOCK

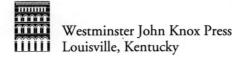
Westminster John Knox Press
Louisville, Kentucky

Book design by Publishers' WorkGroup
Cover design by Drew Stevens

First edition
Published by Westminster John Knox Press
Louisville, Kentucky

This book is printed on acid-free paper that meets the American National Standards Institute Z39.48 standard. ♾

PRINTED IN THE UNITED STATES OF AMERICA
95 96 97 98 99 00 01 02 03 04 — 10 9 8 7 6 5 4 3 2 1

Library of Congress Cataloging-in-Publication Data

Craddock, Fred B.
First and Second Peter and Jude / Fred B. Craddock. — 1st ed.
    p.   cm. — (Westminster Bible companion)
Includes bibliographical references (p.).
ISBN 0-664-25265-6 (alk. paper)
    1. Bible. N.T. Peter—Commentaries. 2. Bible. N.T. Jude—Commentaries. I. Title. II. Series
BS2795.3.C69 1995
227'.92077—dc20   95-19655

Contents

Series Foreword

This series of study guides to the Bible is offered to the church and more specifically to the laity. In daily devotions, in church school classes, and in listening to the preached word, individual Christians turn to the Bible for a sustaining word, a challenging word, and a sense of direction. The word that scripture brings may be highly personal as one deals with the demands and surprises, the joys and sorrows, of daily life. It also may have broader dimensions as people wrestle with moral and theological issues that involve us all. In every congregation and denomination, controversies arise that send ministry and laity alike back to the Word of God to find direction for dealing with difficult matters that confront us.

A significant number of lay women and men in the church also find themselves called to the service of teaching. Most of the time they will be teaching the Bible. In many churches, the primary sustained attention to the Bible and the discovery of its riches for our lives have come from the ongoing teaching of the Bible by persons who have not engaged in formal theological education. They have been willing, and often eager, to study the Bible in order to help others drink from its living water.

This volume is part of a series of books, the Westminster Bible Companion, intended to help the laity of the church read the Bible more clearly and intelligently. Whether such reading is for personal direction or for the teaching of others, the reader cannot avoid the difficulties of trying to understand these words from long ago. The scriptures are clear and clearly available to everyone as they call us to faith in the God who is revealed in Jesus Christ and as they offer to every human being the word of salvation. No companion volumes are necessary in order to hear such words truly. Yet every reader of scripture who pauses to ponder and think further about any text has questions that are not immediately answerable simply by reading the text of scripture. Such questions may be about historical and geographical details or about words that are obscure or so loaded with meaning that one cannot tell at a glance what is at stake. They may be about the fundamental meaning of a passage or about what connection a particular text might have to our contemporary world. Or a teacher preparing for a church school class may simply want to know: What should I say about this biblical passage when I have to teach it next Sunday? It is our hope that these volumes, written by teachers and pastors with long experience studying and teaching the Bible in the church, will help members of the church who want and need to study the Bible with their questions.

The New Revised Standard Version of the Bible is the basis for the interpretive comments that each author provides. The NRSV text is presented at the beginning of the discussion so that the reader may have at hand in a single volume both the scripture passage and the exposition of its meaning. In some instances, where inclusion of the entire passage is not necessary for understanding either the text or the interpreter's discussion, the presentation of the NRSV text may be abbreviated. Usually, the whole of the biblical text is given.

We hope this series will serve the community of faith, opening the Word of God to all the people so that they may be sustained and guided by it.

Introduction

The reader with an active curiosity may have questions about these three writings as a group, prior to the study of each of them individually. For example, is there any particular reason why these books are treated in this one volume? Is it simply a practical matter of joining three small writings in order to approximate in size, if not importance, some of the other New Testament books? And is the reader to assume that this combination of writings, and in this order, will have a bearing on the understanding of the contents of each? In other words, will a person be encouraged to move back and forth among the three in an effort to grasp the meaning of a particular passage?

That 1 and 2 Peter would appear together is, on the face of it, quite obvious. After all, both bear the name of Peter as author (1 Peter 1:1; 2 Peter 1:1), and the second speaks of an earlier letter: "This is now, beloved, the second letter I am writing to you" (2 Peter 3:1). However, in the comments that follow, the relationship between the two may not be as clear as it may seem at first. The signatures are different. The first letter is signed "Peter, an apostle of Jesus Christ" while the second is from "Simeon Peter, a servant and apostle of Jesus Christ." This is a rare occurrence of the word "Simeon" (or Symeon) to refer to the apostle we know as Simon Peter (John 1:40–42), the one other reference appearing at Acts 15:14 in a speech by James the brother of Jesus.

Likewise, the readers of the letters are addressed differently. The first letter is sent "To the exiles of the Dispersion in Pontus, Galatia, Cappadocia, Asia, and Bithynia" (1:1), the second "To those who have received a faith as precious as ours" (1:1). Furthermore, when the second letter reminds the reader of the content of the former (2 Peter 3:1–4), the reference corresponds only in a broad and general way to one of the themes in 1 Peter. This fact alerts us to the possibility that 2 Peter is referring to a prior letter that we no longer possess. We are in possession of a number of writings, whole or fragmentary, not in the New Testament that bear the name of Peter (the *Gospel of Peter*, the *Preaching of Peter*, the *Apocalypse of Peter*, the *Acts of Peter*, the *Epistle of Peter to Philip*, among others) but that are of dates too late and contents too different to be located alongside the Petrine letters in the New Testament. If 2 Peter 3 is referring to a letter now lost to us, the case is certainly not unique. For example, Paul wrote to the Corinthians in what we call his first epistle, "I wrote to you in my letter" (1 Cor. 5:9), clearly a reference to earlier correspondence no longer available to us.

What, then, do these observations mean for our study of these two letters? Two thoughts come immediately to mind. First, the differences between 1 and 2 Peter prompt us to read and to study each as having its own purpose and message. We do not expect the other to jump in and clarify difficult passages for us. This is to say, we will not expect that messages in 1 Peter will be completed or modified in 2 Peter, nor will we assume that 2 Peter presupposes a knowledge of 1 Peter.

Second, here as elsewhere in Bible study, one sometimes says, "We do not know." This is the honest acknowledgment of the brightest scholar as well as the beginning student of scripture. The recipients of these letters very likely understood every word they heard (letters were read aloud in the churches) because this mail was to them and about them. But imagine if you were to find beside the path a letter that reads:

Dear Harry,

We are hoping Frank will be released by the weekend. Mollie can hardly wait. The old gang is planning the usual party at Charlie's place. Please bring Tracy. See you there.

Peggy

You and I do not know these people. We do not know who is in "the old gang." We have no address for Charlie's place. We do not even know if Frank is in the hospital, the army, or prison. But Harry and Peggy know, and without the aid of commentaries. So it was with the writers and receivers of letters in the New Testament. We read carefully, we do background research, we speculate, and still sometimes we say, "We do not know."

We do so reluctantly because faith wants to understand. We do not agree with those who say that believing is what we do when we do not understand. Such a view champions anti-intellectualism in the service of faith. Even so, some of the history surrounding readers, writers, and particular contexts of New Testament writings is no longer retrievable. We hunger for any new information, and our probing will never stop, but our not knowing is not fatal. While reading scripture is often an experience of distance, of being aware of long ago and far away, it is also an experience of intimacy. The Holy Spirit operating in the text and in the reader join in generating and regenerating faith. Thus, we enter into the study of these three letters with that expectation.

There remains the question as to why Jude is placed in this volume along with the letters of Peter. Jude does not follow 1 and 2 Peter in the order of books in the New Testament, and if the question is simply a practical one of combining small writings, then why not 1, 2, 3 John and Jude? The answer will come with even a casual reading of the epistle of Jude. The content of Jude is unusually similar to that of 2 Peter, especially chapter 2. In fact, in its central message 2 Peter is much closer to Jude than to 1 Peter. Therefore, while the epistles of Peter offer little help in interpreting each other, Jude will aid in understanding 2 Peter, and vice versa.

Having said this about the relationship, or lack thereof, among these three writings, it is well to remind ourselves that they have a common literary heritage in that all three are letters. The letter, or epistle, is the most common literary form in the New Testament, 21 of the 27 books being, at least partially, in epistolary style. Even the Revelation to John is actually a pastoral letter to seven churches in Asia Minor. The nature of the epistolary form and its significance for understanding the content will become evident in the discussion of each letter.

And, finally, these three writings belong to that group of epistles called "general" or "catholic." In the New Testament there are seven: James, 1 and 2 Peter, 1, 2, and 3 John, and Jude. They are called general or catholic (universal) epistles because they are addressed to the church at large or, at least, to the church scattered over a wide geographical area. By contrast, Paul's letters are to particular congregations or persons. Naturally one would expect to find in a general letter a lack of specific details about the readers and their situations. Likewise, general letters reflect a relationship between writers and readers quite different from that exhibited in Paul's letters to friends and to congregations he knew quite well. Who would dare, who would have the authority to address with words of command, correction, and pastoral oversight, "the church at large?" Obviously general epistles reflect a time and place in which certain leaders assumed a normative influence over the church as church and not merely over congregations to which they had ministered. And because these letters are to readers with no particular address, their titles do not bear the names of the recipients, as do Paul's, but rather those of the senders; that is, Peter, Jude, James, and John.

First Peter

Introduction

The purpose of an introduction is to orient, not indoctrinate. The key is to help readers enter the book and find their way without telling them what to find there. One does not want to give the impression that all discoveries have already been made. Readers properly expect such information as will aid in listening to the text but not a predetermination as to what is to be heard. Many introductions give the impression of placing conclusions up front, and that impression is difficult to avoid. A case could be made for placing an "introduction" at the end, the reader being then in better position to assess the merits of what the commentator says about authorship, date, purpose, literary character, and central message of the book. Obviously I observe the traditional location of the introduction here, but with an effort to be more invitational to the reader, guiding rather than taking over your responsibility; that is, to engage the text and in it to listen for God's Word. After all, in 1 Peter we are all called "priests" (2:5) and that means each of us is to study, to worship, and to minister before God. Peter refers to himself as an elder among elders (5:1); the writer of this commentary is a student among students.

WHAT WE ALREADY KNOW

Most of us do not approach a book as total strangers even though we would probably respond to the question, "What do you know about 1 Peter?" with one word: "Nothing." But such a question asks for recall, and few of us have good recall. First Peter has appeared in sermons, Sunday school lessons, and perhaps as tidbits in conversation, but who can recall it, or even identify a partially familiar term or phrase as coming from 1 Peter? So much for recall. But recognition is another matter. Once one begins to read 1 Peter, names, words, or even verses that lie beyond the reach of recall are recognized. Yes, we have heard or read that before. So, to dispel the initial sense of strangeness, read this letter in its entirety, pausing to enjoy every moment of recognition.

What persons appear here whom we have met before? We begin, of course, with Jesus, but that Jesus is the central figure in a New Testament letter cannot be automatically assumed. In James, for instance, Jesus is mentioned only twice, and in Paul's letters the Jesus we meet is primarily Jesus crucified and raised from the dead. In 1 Peter, however, the reader encounters not only the crucified and risen Jesus but also the Jesus who in his lifetime provided a model of behavior in the face of verbal and physical abuse.

Three familiar figures from Hebrew scriptures appear: Abraham and Sarah (3:6) who by trust and obedience to God's call became the father and mother of all who believe, and Noah (3:20) whose ark was a symbol of God's salvation in a world of disobedience and violence. In addition, three persons whom we meet elsewhere in the New Testament reappear in this letter. First is Simon Peter whose name occurs as the signature on this letter (1:1). Simon was one of the first disciples chosen by Jesus (Mark 1:16–20), the name Peter (Cephas in Aramaic, a Semitic language related to Hebrew, widely spoken in the Near East and very likely the language of Jesus) being given him by Jesus (John 1:41–42). His career is traced in the Gospels and Acts. In fact, after Jesus and Paul, Peter is the most visible figure in the New Testament. Secondly, there is Silvanus (a Latinized form of Silas), Peter's secretary or courier (the text does not make it fully clear in which capacity he served, 5:12). The mention of Silas is surprising since he appears often in Acts and in Paul's letters as a missionary companion of Paul (Acts 15:40–18:5; 2 Cor. 1:19; 1 Thess. 1:1). And finally, 1 Peter mentions "my son Mark" (5:13). Assuming all the New Testament references to Mark are to the same person, we know him as the son of a disciple in Jerusalem named Mary (Acts 12:12), as a companion of Paul and of Barnabas (Acts 12:25; 13:5, 13; 15:36–40) and as one who, after an early dispute, became very close to Paul (Col. 4:10; 2 Tim. 4:11; Philemon 24). Later tradition identifies Mark as the author of the second Gospel, an account which was, says the tradition, Mark's recollection of the preaching of Peter in Rome.

Are there places mentioned that the reader recognizes? Of the five provinces listed in the address (1:1), very likely Galatia is familiar since Paul addressed one of his letters to the churches there. Less likely, but perhaps Asia is remembered as the destination of the Revelation to John: "to the seven churches that are in Asia" (Rev. 1:4). However, a good guess would be that many readers recognize the name of the city from which 1 Peter was sent: Babylon (5:13), again because of its frequent and dramatic appearance in Revelation (14:8; 16:19; 17:5; 18:2, 10, 21). Readers of 1 Peter and Revelation understood Babylon to refer to Rome, the center of power which at times could (and did) pose a threat to Christian communities. In subsequent generations, church leaders have used the name Babylon as a designation for any major city or country considered to be a center of forces for evil.

And finally, does the reader of 1 Peter recognize terms or themes that are contributed by this book to the general pool of Christian ideas or beliefs? Surprisingly, there are more than may have been anticipated. In this letter the term "Christian" appears (4:16), there being only two other uses in the New Testament (Acts 11:26; 26:28). From 1 Peter, Charles M. Sheldon drew the phrase "in his steps" (2:21) for the title of his once immensely popular book on Christian morality. Here followers of Jesus are addressed as aliens, and exiles (1:1; 2:11), self-designations in common currency whenever and wherever believers have felt "not at home" in the world. Christians are also those born again (1:3, 23). In those times and places in which the church accents the suffering rather than solely the death of Christ, 1 Peter is a primary source. Forms of the word translated "suffering," from which we get "pathos," "paschal" (as in paschal or passover lamb), and later the latinized "passion" appear 16 times in this letter (for example, 2:19, 21, 23; 3:17, 18; 4:15) as central to the understanding of what it means to be a Christian. To the church's sacramental life this letter contributes a major statement on baptism (3:18–22) and to the Apostles' Creed 1 Peter gives the strange to modern ears but always important affirmation of the work of Christ, "he descended into hell" (3:19–20).

These and other items of recognition or near recognition can function for the reader in two very positive ways: (1) they can reduce the inhibiting sense of strangeness when walking through this letter; and (2) they can stir the curiosity to ask further important and specific questions of the text. Contrary to a widely held opinion, a healthy curiosity is not the enemy but the friend of Bible study and of Christian faith.

WHAT WE WISH TO KNOW

Certainly one person cannot speak for another on the subject of what we wish to know; experience, prior knowledge, and circumstances generate in each of us certain questions. However, some matters are of such broad significance that to suggest them may aid all of us in this study while leaving to each person individual pursuits which, I hope, will come to helpful ends.

One thing we wish to know is, who is Jesus Christ portrayed in this letter? This is not primarily a historical question; we are continually faced with the question, who is Jesus Christ for us today? and 1 Peter lies among the authoritative sources from which we seek answers. Will we meet here a Christ who is primarily a cosmic figure, exalted at God's right hand and holding authority over all created life, visible and invisible? Or perhaps the writer has seen fit to hold before the readers a risen-from-the-dead Christ, giving us essentially an Easter message. Or is the reader to receive a word from Good Friday, a proclamation of the meaning and benefits of Christ's death on the cross? Or possibly we will meet here more of what the Gospels offer, sayings of Jesus and stories about his earthly ministry. In fact, this is a realistic expectation since the letter bears the name of Simon Peter. What would be more natural than to recall for believers in Asia Minor what Jesus of Nazareth said and did in Galilee and on his way to Jerusalem? To do so would not only be appropriate for the readers but a proper stewardship of Peter's firsthand experiences of Jesus.

This line of thought naturally raises the question of the relationship between the writer and the readers. This matter is primary in understanding any correspondence. The writer is identified as Peter (1:1) writing from Rome (Babylon, 5:13), and the tradition that Peter went to Rome and was martyred there in the time of Nero (A.D. 54–68) is quite strong. But did he know Christians in five provinces of western and northern Asia Minor? Although Paul was a missionary in Asia Minor, we have no record of Peter going there. We know from the New Testament that Peter traveled along the coast of Palestine (Acts 9:32–10:48), up to Antioch of Syria (Gal. 2:11), and perhaps to Corinth (1 Cor. 1:12; 9:5). If the writer was not known directly by the readers, then the right or authority of the one writing such a letter to those churches is a reasonable question to raise. After all, we want as much as possible to hear the letter as they did.

This means, of course, we want to know the recipients. They are obviously Christians, but are they Jewish or Gentile in background, or some of both? Are they new in the faith and therefore in need of further orientation and instruction, or have they been believers long enough to be falling into discouragement and apathy? Are the churches in which they work and worship living in harmony or in discord? And in what social and political conditions are those believers seeking to be faithful? Both public rejection and public embrace can be problems for the church, but they call for very different messages.

All of this is to ask, what was it to be Christian in the time and place of those first readers? The extent to which we can know that will be the extent to which we can listen to the letter for ourselves. The Christian life has been variously defined as right worship, right believing, or right living. Is the writer inclined toward one of these perspectives more than the others? And what resources were available to the readers to aid them in living together as faith communities and in making moral and ethical choices as minorities in that culture? We want to know if they had recourse to Old Testament texts, or to sayings of Jesus, or to the example of Jesus, or to apostolic rulings, or to revelations of inspired prophets, or to congregational consensus, or to the leading of the Holy Spirit, or to strong moral voices in the larger culture. On such matters we are not simply curious; we are anxious for help in our own relationships and decision making. In listening to 1 Peter, we will, of course, be overhearing, but it is no secret that our desire is to hear a word to us.

A WAY TO BEGIN

I offer the following perspective on 1 Peter as a place to stand when reading the book, a view of the forest before exploring the trees. You should, of course, after studying the text feel free to modify or reject any portion of this perspective that the content itself seems not to support. When one comes upon any writing, whether on a library shelf, in a trunk in the attic, or between the covers of an "anthology" like the Bible, the document is first examined with several fundamental questions in mind. We now ask those questions and answer them to the extent that they can be answered.

What Kind of Literature Is It?

First Peter is a letter. We know the rather standard form for letters in the world of early Christianity. Cicero wrote more than 900 letters; Pliny, a young governor in the service of the emperor Trajan, wrote more than 60 letters to his superior; Paul wrote many letters to churches; countless others wrote letters, both private and public, which are still available from that ancient time. The form, sometimes abbreviated, sometimes expanded, was as follows: signature of the writer; person or persons addressed; greeting; a word of praise or thanksgiving; the message; closing greeting; farewell. Clearly 1 Peter conforms to this pattern. In its nature one could say that this letter comes somewhere between public and private. It is public not in the sense that it was to be posted on a bulletin board on a city street but in that it was to be read aloud in Christian assemblies located in five provinces of Asia Minor. It is private not in the sense that it is to one person but rather in that it is to one kind of person, the one whose trust in God is shaped by commitment to Jesus Christ. In fact, because the letter is to Christians in different provinces spread over 129,000 square miles, we cannot expect references to specific circumstances that would not pertain to all the readers. The letter circulated from province to province; some have suggested that the order of the list in 1:1 may indicate the route of the epistle.

It is only fair to acknowledge that some students of 1 Peter have questioned its epistolary character, primarily on two grounds. The first is that it contains materials more liturgical and homiletical than one would expect in a letter. Very likely passages such as 2:21–24 and 3:18–22 are hymns or confessions of faith, but the quotation of worship materials by the author is of insufficient quantity to justify calling 1 Peter a baptismal liturgy thinly disguised as a letter. And likewise there are in the letter elements one finds in homilies: instruction, warning, encouragement, and exhortation, but their presence does not destroy the epistolary nature of the writing. Recall letters of Paul about which there is no dispute; he quotes hymns (Phil. 2:6–11; Col. 1:15–20) and creeds (1 Cor. 8:6; 2 Cor. 8:9) and he exhorts, cajoles, warns, instructs, and encourages. After all, what is a Christian leader supposed to do and say in a letter to a congregation?

The second ground for questioning the epistolary character of 1 Peter lies in the sometimes awkward transitions. Admittedly, outlining 1 Peter is difficult and translators puzzle over where to begin and end paragraphs, but again, the same is true of Paul's letters. Perhaps the most unusual point of transition is at 4:12. The NRSV adds space between 4:11 and 12, but is it necessary to assume, as do some, that 4:12ff. was added later by the same or a different writer in order to address a new and catastrophic situation not known when 1:3–4:11 was written? No; in fact, in the study that follows I will show that 4:12ff. simply presents a new image not a new time or change of circumstance.

What is important as you read is to keep in mind the primary functions of a letter. A letter, to be sure, conveys a message, but two other vital purposes are served. First, by means of the letter the absent writer is made present to the reader. And second, the letter services a relationship between the writer and the reader, a relationship that is initiated, nourished, or altered by the correspondence. The text itself will inform us on the details of these three functions.

Who Wrote the Letter?

The writer is identified as Peter, an apostle (1:1), a fellow elder and a witness of the sufferings of Christ (5:1). For centuries, students of the letter have wondered how an uneducated Galilean fisherman (Acts 4:13) could write Greek of this quality. Some respond with the observation that "Through Silvanus . . . I have written" (5:12) may mean that Silvanus served as secretary rather than simply the courier. However, discussing Peter's literary abilities leads nowhere.

Equally unfruitful are the attempts to attribute this letter to Paul. It has similarities to Pauline letters, especially Romans, but affinities to Hebrews and James are no less striking. Most likely, common traditions lie back of all of them.

More helpful to our study is the question of Simon Peter's relation to churches in an area we usually associate with Paul's mission, churches that were, as we shall note below, heavily Gentile in membership. Paul referred to Peter as "an apostle to the circumcised" (Gal. 2:8), but Acts reports on Peter's preaching to Gentiles (chaps. 10—11, 15). And a letter need not imply a prior relationship between the writer and the reader; a letter may serve to initiate a relationship.

Arguing for or against Petrine authorship has lost its importance for most students of this letter. We now know that the name of a significant leader such as Peter or Paul or John was preserved and used by persons who were in the circle of that person's influence and who wished to continue the life and tradition of that leader. This letter represents the teaching and preaching of Simon Peter and extends that ministry into Asia Minor, whether or not Simon penned it, dictated it, or was the source of the content used by a follower of his. In fact, thinking of it in terms of private correspondence is probably a bit unfair to the letter. The churches in Asia Minor are greeted by a fellow elder (5:1), a brother (Silvanus), a son (Mark), and a sister (the church in Rome). One has the sense of a house-to-house, family-to-family, church-to-church relationship initiated by this letter.

To Whom Was the Letter Written?

The addressees are "exiles of the Dispersion" (1:1), Christian communities scattered throughout five provinces at the eastern extremity of the Roman Empire. We do not know who, other than Paul, first brought the gospel to these regions. According to Acts 2:9, persons from Pontus, Asia, and Cappadocia were present in Jerusalem on Pentecost; perhaps they brought Christianity back to Asia Minor. Neither do we know how large the churches were. The historian Ramsay MacMullen has estimated there were at the close of the first century about 40,000 believers in an empire of 70 million, a minority even where the churches thrived. We do know they were identified in the society by a name, "Christian" (1 Peter 4:16), and wearing that name brought social ostracism and various kinds of abuse.

Unlike the persons addressed in Hebrews who have been believers for some time (5:12–14), the Christians here seem to be new to the faith. Baptism occurred in the recent past: "Now that you have purified your souls by your obedience to the truth" (1:22; also 3:18–22); "like newborn infants, long for the pure, spiritual milk" (2:2). The contrasts common to conversion language ("formerly you were . . . but now") also testify to rather new experiences of discipleship: no hope/true hope (1:21), slavery/freedom (1:18), ignorance/knowledge (1:14), flesh/spirit (4:6), death/life (1:3; 4:6), disobedience/obedience (1:22), not God's people/God's people (2:10). This fact, coupled with a Gentile (1:14, 18; 2:10) rather than Jewish background, meant that many in the churches were too young in faith to be adequate for the hardships they were enduring. However, as we shall see, the writer assumed the readers knew the Hebrew scriptures (in Greek translation), a knowledge that may have come through catechism for those seeking membership, a process that may have taken a year or more.

That the Christians of Asia Minor were suffering persecution is quite clear from the letter, but there is no evidence in the text that an official Roman persecution is underway. Nero's violence against Christians (A.D. 64–68) was confined to Rome; under Domitian (A.D. 81–96) some Christians were killed (Rev. 2:13); and during Trajan's reign (A.D. 98–117), Pliny, governor in Pontus and Bithynia, responded to citizens' complaints against Christians and after interrogations executed some for refusal to deny Jesus as Lord and worship the emperor. However, official empire-wide decrees against Christians did not begin until the time of Decius (A.D. 249–51).

First Peter reflects the kind of persecution inflicted by the citizenry, not the government, persecution that involved social ostracism and verbal abuse ("maligned," 2:12; 3:16; "reviled," 4:14; "abused," 2:23; 3:9). Christ's suffering and not his death is the model held before the readers. This is to say, there is no call for martyrdom; rather the mistreatment to be endured seems to correspond to that of Christians elsewhere (Acts 19:23–40;

1 Thess. 2:14; Heb. 10:32–34; James 1:2–3). None of these remarks is intended to make light of the pain these Christians suffered. Sometimes hate mail, anonymous phone calls, ugly epithets spray painted on the garage door, social slights, bodily threats, and the segregation or isolation of one's children can amount to greater cruelty than the clearly defined opposition of a government.

For What Purpose Was the Letter Written?

Clearly 1 Peter was written to encourage the Christians of Asia Minor, to call them to confidence in the power of God, to renew hope, to help them find meaning in their suffering, and to urge them to stay together in mutual support. Leaders in the congregations are reminded of their responsibilities as shepherds of the flock during these difficult times. The new converts need help in understanding how to respond to their former way of life with its relationships and institutions and how to apply the gospel to marriage and family and the workplace. Instruction is given in these matters, and, not surprisingly, the writer reveals the same difficulty we have in giving definition and identity to the church in society. Tension is there, to be sure, between the believers and their culture. Repeatedly the readers are reminded that they are pilgrims, exiles, aliens in the world, but in the household of God they have a new family, a new home. Even so, how does this new family relate to governing authorities and social institutions with which they must deal every day? And how does the church respond to a society that is making life miserable for Christians?

In brief, how are believers to remain in tension with a nonbelieving culture and yet relate to that culture in such ways as will gain favorable report and new converts to the faith? The writer seeks to move beyond missionary strategy (what will work) to an authentic presentation of the way of Christ in the world, the Christ in whose steps they are to walk. All this sounds clearly familiar, and in reading, distances collapse and 1 Peter seems written to us.

Some students of 1 Peter find an implicit purpose to the letter in the fact that it came from Rome. They suggest that a word from Christians in the capital city calling for peaceful relations with society and respect for government might carry more authority and be more effective in its urging than a letter from another quarter. After all, the church in Rome had double apostolic association, with both Paul and Peter. And in return, peace in Asia Minor could have positive results for Christians in Rome. However, at the time of this letter (variously dated between A.D. 64 and

90) the church in Rome may not have yet ascended in prestige above other churches. Before many decades, however, the claim of double apostolic authority would be the basis for the Roman church's extension of its influence to other churches.

OUTLINE OF FIRST PETER

As I stated earlier, many readers of 1 Peter have had difficulty following the flow of thought, given the sudden transitions and the amount of quoted material. In a recent study of this problem, Troy Martin (*Metaphor and Composition in 1 Peter*) has suggested that the principle of composition might not be linear thinking in developing themes but rather the clustering of ideas around key metaphors or images. His proposal seems helpful for our purposes and will, with a number of modifications, provide the structure for our study of the text. The commentary will be framed on the following outline:

Salutation   1:1–2
The Blessing   1:3–12
Christians as the Household of God   1:13–2:10
    As Children with a New Father   1:13–21
    As Children with New Brothers and Sisters   1:22–2:3
    Forming a New Temple of God   2:4–10
Christians as Aliens in the World   2:11–3:12
    Aliens Both Transient and Resident   2:11–12
    Under Authority Yet Free   2:13–17
    A Particular Word to Slaves   2:18–25
    A Particular Word to Wives   3:1–6
    A Particular Word to Husbands   3:7
    And a Word to All   3:8–12
Christians as Sufferers in the World   3:13–5:11
    While Doing What is Right   3:13–17
    Defined by the Passion and Resurrection of Jesus   3:18–4:2
    Living in the Will of God   4:3–11
    As Christ's Partners in Both Suffering and Glory   4:12–19
    The Elders Bear Special Responsibility   5:1–5a
    A Closing Exhortation to All   5:5b–11
Greetings   5:12–14a
Farewell   5:14b

Commentary

SALUTATION
1 Peter 1:1–2

> 1:1 **Peter, an apostle of Jesus Christ, To the exiles of the Dispersion in Pon-tus, Galatia, Cappadocia, Asia, and Bithynia,** 2 **who have been chosen and destined by God the Father and sanctified by the Spirit to be obedient to Je-sus Christ and to be sprinkled with his blood:**
> **May grace and peace be yours in abundance.**

Having discussed in the Introduction matters of authorship, the recipi-ents, and the form of an early Christian letter, we are now ready to hear the extraordinary way in which the writer defines and greets the readers. They are geographically located, to be sure, and this is not an unimpor-tant bit of information. After all, they and all God's people are called to be faithful in a specific time and place in history. To pretend otherwise out of some erroneous view of "spirituality" is to deny the historical na-ture of both Judaism and Christianity and to forget that God's central act of self-revelation was in Jesus, a man of Nazareth in Galilee, born of woman, who suffered under Pontius Pilate. However, time and place do not fully define anyone, and especially those who trust in God. Therefore the author reminds his readers who they really are by means of six very important terms.

Exiles

As used here, "exiles" refers to persons who are temporary or transient res-idents in a land not their own. The term has a long history as a means of political punishment, but there is no hint here that the Christians ad-dressed have been banished to this geographical area. Rather, they are ex-iles in the sense of not being fully at home in their environment, of being without the rights and privileges of citizens. Abraham, seeking a small plot for burying Sarah, made his request as a stranger (exile) and alien among his neighbors (Gen. 23:4; see also Heb. 11:13). The psalmist, asking for God's favor, does so as "passing guest, an alien, like all my forebears" (Psalm 39:12). As Phil. 3:20; Heb. 11:13–16, and countless chapters of subsequent church history make clear, the Christian as exile became a useful and widely embraced image. One needs to be on guard, however, against two dangers that lurk in the word "exile" and associated behavior. The first danger is that in order to claim the term and its implications, some may deliberately irritate or in various ways attack the society in which they live, drawing its fire and enjoying the suffering that follows. A clear tension over different value systems is to be expected; it comes with the commitment; but Jesus asks no one to go looking for a cross. The second danger is that people may be socially and politically irresponsible on the ground that they are exiles. To invest nothing in the care of the earth and of all God's children for whom Christ died has absolutely no precedent in the life and work of Jesus. Rendering to Caesar and to God is in every situation a judgment call, but to relinquish either is to abandon the tension that is an ingredient of the life of faith.

Of the Dispersion

The Dispersion (or Diaspora, meaning "scattered") was already a designation for those Jews scattered among many nations after the loss of Palestine to foreign powers. The expression is so used in the New Testament (John 7:35), but the church adopted the term symbolically as a description of its own place in the world (James 1:1). It is both a compliment to a church that took seriously its missionary mandate to go to all nations and a description of the "at home, not at home" status of the church in the world.

What is important for Christians to understand is that the term provides continuity between Judaism and Christianity. Both words, "exile" and "Dispersion," evoke memories of Israel, its history, faith, writings, and rituals of worship. The writer of 1 Peter will assume on the part of the Gentile Christian readers not only a knowledge of the Hebrew scriptures but a sense of kinship with Israel. For too long many Christians have accented discontinuity between the synagogue and the church, as though there had been a change of God's plan or as though the identity of the church could be established only by attacks on its mother. Flaws and failures existed in Israel's life as they do in the church; Jesus was not hesitant to call for radical reform. However, Jesus, Paul, Luke, and others continually spoke of the single purpose of God from creation until now, embracing both Jew and Gentile. It is foolish to chop down the family tree.

Chosen

How extraordinary that scattered exiles would be called the chosen ones! In the traditional language of faith, these are the "elect." The word makes no room for elitism or arrogance, for such attitudes imply that one is chosen because of superior qualities. Not so. Jacob was chosen over his twin Esau before birth, squelching any notion of merit. Israel was chosen from among rich and powerful nations, putting the lie to thoughts of superiority. To call the roll of the chosen is to abandon the idea that reasons for the choice lay in the persons themselves.

Rather, the word reminds us of the initiative of God, that we are who we are by the prior act of God. We may think of ourselves as the searchers but actually we are the found. We may seek to know, but our life is in being known of God. That we are chosen affirms first of all the freedom of God, which is the necessary precondition of grace. That we are chosen also affirms that our lives are from and in God. The identity of the church is neither given nor withdrawn by a threatening government or hassling neighbors. This encouragement, this support is at all times vital but never more so than when the chosen are daily badgered, suffer verbal abuse and threat of bodily harm, and are constantly reminded that they are socially and politically outsiders. It takes but one trip to the microphone at a public gathering to express values born of the gospel to make 1 Peter read like a personal letter.

But again, let us warn ourselves against translating "chosen" as "exclusive." A God who chooses each chooses all. Imagine a child being told by the ticketmaster at the circus that free admission will be given tomorrow at the afternoon performance. "I will be admitted free" is the one exciting thought of that young mind. The next afternoon the child is invited into the tent, along with dozens of other children. The child enters but is crestfallen, no longer feeling special. Does the free admission of many make any one of them less chosen? Of course not, but it could feel that way.

Destined

Perhaps no word could offer more assurance and encouragement to small churches scattered in an unfriendly environment than this: "destined by

God the Father." Literally the term here is "foreknown" and belongs to a cluster of words that affirm and celebrate the working out of God's purpose for the world. Recall, for example, from Eph. 1:4–5: "He chose us in Christ before the foundation of the world to be holy and blameless before him in love. He destined us for adoption as his children." Perhaps the classic locus for this language is Rom. 8:29–30: "foreknew," "predestined," "called," "justified," "glorified." The experience of the believer (called and justified) is set in the grand movement of God's will, from foreknowledge to glorification. Human decisions and responsibility are not eliminated, but neither is God's purpose totally dependent on what we do and say.

Both Judaism and Christianity expressed this belief with the phrase "before the foundation of the world." This is the language of assurance for the people of God. Hermas, a Christian writer of the next generation, encouraged believers by describing the church as existing before the world was made. Joachim Jeremias, a German scholar, once told of a visit to the backyard tent of a Jewish friend celebrating the Feast of Tabernacles, which is a time to remember Israel's tent life in the desert. Fastened to the door of the tent were two slips of paper with the words "From God" and "To God." The conviction of one's origin and destination makes the pilgrim life not only endurable, but one of praise and thanksgiving.

Sanctified

Again the writer speaks not of what the readers are doing or are supposed to do but rather of what is done to and for them. One activity of the Holy Spirit is the sanctifying or hallowing of God's people. The exact wording here is found also at 2 Thess. 2:13. Paul's favorite use of the word was in its noun form: the "saints," a term for addressing the churches (Rom. 1:7; 1 Cor. 1:2; 2 Cor. 1:1; Phil. 1:1). In the language of the Lord's Prayer, the common translation is "hallowed." It is regrettable that the terms "saint" and "sanctified" have in popular usage been reserved for that rare person whose life is so near moral and benevolent perfection as to be held at a distance in awe. Of course, those who trust in God are to manifest the same in character and good works, but this is the expected behavior of the whole church, not of a special few. Even so, the accent is not on our moral achievement but on the activity of God through the Holy Spirit. Paul called the Corinthians saints and then proceeded to address a tub full of problems in that church. Saints? Yes, because the Spirit had set them apart for God. However, in the process of Christian maturing, the sanctifying action of the Spirit does actually become a quality of character, the believer reflecting something of the nature of God in acts and relationships that further the purpose of God.

Obedient and Sprinkled with His Blood

I treat "obedient to Christ" and "sprinkled with his blood" as one expression because they recall a single act of covenant making. The writer again assumes that his readers have a knowledge of the Old Testament, in this case Exodus 24. Israel had received God's law at Sinai. Moses read the book of the covenant and the people pledged to be obedient. Moses then sealed the covenant by sprinkling on the people the blood of an ox. This sprinkling with blood has a significance different from both the Passover rite of blood on the door and the Day of Atonement act of pouring blood on the ark of the covenant.

To be sure, the New Testament interprets the death of Christ against the background of both Passover and the Day of Atonement, but here the association is most likely to covenant and obedience. The writer may have in mind and may be evoking the readers' recent baptism and pledge of obedience to Christ.

The three-fold nature of the statement—destined by God, sanctified by the Spirit, sprinkled with the blood of Christ—has a formal ring to it (recall Matt. 28:19, baptism in the name of the Father, Son, and Holy Spirit) and suggests liturgical use.

All that has been said thus far is the author's description of the recipients, reminding them of who they really are. The greeting proper is very brief, though not so brief as the common greeting in letters of that day, which consisted of one word: Greetings (Acts 15:23; James 1:1). Here the double greeting "grace and peace" may reflect Pauline influence, this being Paul's usual way of greeting the churches. The additional "in abundance" is a typical Jewish expression, lifting whatever is said to the level of the superlative; literally, "be multiplied."

Both grace and peace are fleshed out in the remainder of the letter, but a few remarks are in order here. "Grace" is a variation on a common secular word of greeting. The church turned it into a special greeting for grace is divine favor, unmerited blessing, God's yes, the initiative of God's love. It precedes all divine imperatives and human response. Preceding the Ten Commandments was the word of God's favor; preceding Christ's instructions in the Sermon on the Mount was the word of God's favor or beatitude. "Grace" is the central word of our faith and the root of the word (*charis*) gives us also joy, gratitude, and a name for the sacrament of the table, Eucharist. "Peace," or *shalom*, is drawn from the treasury of Judaism. It describes a state of harmony or balance of power and may characterize one's inner life, one's relation to others, or one's relation to God. To a church unsettled by its circumstances, it is a most welcome blessing.

And it is not coincidental that the two words of greeting join two heritages: "grace" from the Gentile culture, "peace" from the Jewish. In only two words, God's unifying act in Christ is recalled and all its beneficiaries renew their commitment to it. "For he is our peace; in his flesh he has made both groups into one and has broken down the dividing wall, that is, the hostility between us" (Eph. 2:14). "Grace and peace" say, among other things, that before God there is no difference among us, and the church that truly hears this word lives accordingly.

THE BLESSING
1 Peter 1:3–12

> 1:3 **Blessed be the God and Father of our Lord Jesus Christ! By his great mercy he has given us a new birth into a living hope through the resurrection of Jesus Christ from the dead, 4 and into an inheritance that is imperishable, undefiled, and unfading, kept in heaven for you, 5 who are being protected by the power of God through faith for a salvation ready to be revealed in the last time. 6 In this you rejoice, even if now for a little while you have had to suffer various trials, 7 so that the genuineness of your faith—being more precious than gold that, though perishable, is tested by fire—may be found to result in praise and glory and honor when Jesus Christ is revealed. 8 Although you have not seen him, you love him; and even though you do not see him now, you believe in him and rejoice with an indescribable and glorious joy, 9 for you are receiving the outcome of your faith, the salvation of your souls.**
>
> **10 Concerning this salvation, the prophets who prophesied of the grace that was to be yours made careful search and inquiry, 11 inquiring about the person or time that the Spirit of Christ within them indicated when it testified in advance to the sufferings destined for Christ and the subsequent glory. 12 It was revealed to them that they were serving not themselves but you, in regard to the things that have now been announced to you through those who brought you good news by the Holy Spirit sent from heaven—things into which angels long to look!**

Before we explore the contents of the passage, let us reflect for a moment on the nature of this unit and how it functions. First of all, it is a blessing (eulogy) addressed to God. Most of us are familiar with blessings said at meals, but in these prayers God is petitioned to bless the food. In some restaurants cards on the tables provide Protestant, Catholic, and Jewish blessings. A typical Christian mealtime prayer says, "Bless this food to our bodies' use and us to your service." But notice a Jewish prayer: "Blessed are you, Creator of the universe, for you satisfy the hungry and fill our hearts with good things." The blessing in our text is in the Jewish tradition (See Psalm 66:20; Rom. 1:25; 9:5; 2 Cor. 1:3–7; Eph. 1:3).

Second, this blessing is adapted for use in an epistle. Paul had set the pattern for church letters with a thanksgiving or eulogy immediately following the greeting (Galatians is the exception). This thanksgiving or eulogy was lengthened beyond that of popular correspondence to include in brief phrases and allusions the principal content of the body of the letter. Hence the eulogy or blessing of 1 Peter is long (3–12), consisting of one very complex sentence that has, for the sake of clarity, been translated as several shorter sentences (compare 2 Cor. 1:3–7 and Eph. 1:3–14). And notice how pregnant the blessing is with the great themes of the letter: God's salvation, through the Son, revealed by the Holy Spirit; the suffering of Christ and the church; anticipation of the end time; continuity between the prophets and the gospel; new birth; living hope; eternal inheritance; preaching that generates faith; and angels interested in God's favor toward us. The author overwhelms our capacity to consider so much so swiftly stated, but all these themes will be revisited in the letter. For the present, however, we can see how a blessing becomes a doxology, becomes a statement of faith, becomes a homily, all within ten verses.

Third, the blessing is shaped for the worship of the church. The writer knows that the letter will be read in the assembly of the congregations and, therefore, it has a very clear liturgical character. This means at least three things. First, the language is Godward; God and not only the church is addressed. Second, worship or praise provides the context in which the message of the letter is to be heard. All teaching and preaching properly begin and end in praise of God. And finally, rhetorical flourishes and hyperbolic speech are expected as the appropriate language of worship. How else express the surpassing glory of God, the inclusiveness of God's grace, and the appropriate acts of adoration if not by exaggerated language? "Were the whole realm of nature mine, that were a present far too small." "And I heard the voice of many angels surrounding the throne . . . , they numbered myriads of myriads and thousands of thousands" (Rev. 5:11). Such flourishes are the language of praise. It is not enough to speak only of earth; heaven, too, is involved (1 Peter 1:4, 12). The cast of characters includes not only humans but angels (v. 12). The story line stretches from Israel's prophets to the end of time (vv. 5, 10–12). And the salvation that is ours is a subject that bursts the limits of language and can be presented only in terms of what it is not: it is an inheritance that does not perish, is not defiled, and never fades (v. 4). It is a joy that cannot be described (v. 8).

The NRSV helps the reader with this lengthy and profound blessing by dividing it into two parts, verses 3–9 and 10–12. Perhaps even more helpful is the way the Revised English Bible (REB) handles it by presenting the message in four smaller units: verses 3–5, 6–7, 8–9, and 10–12. The comments that follow are ordered in these four parts.

Verses 3–5 celebrate the activity of God that sweeps from our new birth to the final unveiling of God's salvation, activity that is prompted by the great mercy of God. The benefits of this grace are portrayed in several images. We are given a *new birth*, a description reminiscent of John's Gospel (1:13; 3:3–5) and instructive in its reminder that who and what we are is not of our own doing. This image of new birth (see also 1:23) may allude to the recent, or as some scholars would say, the soon-to-happen baptism of some of the recipients of the letter.

The hope into which we are born is a *divine hope;* that is, a hope which does not simply wait for the end time but is active and vigorous, fueling the life and activity of the believer. Hope is the very stuff of life; it keeps the farmer on the tractor, the prisoner alive, the student at the books, and the patient watching for the morning. Hope fills present sacrifices with joy and keeps us at worthy tasks even though rewards are small and those who say "thank you" are few. This hope is not whistling in the dark nor is it activated only by spring flowers. Rather it is grounded in the resurrection of Jesus Christ.

This birth into the family of God brings also *an inheritance*, not of a promised land (Deut. 15:4) subject to the decay of nature or the fortunes of war, but one "kept in heaven." In the words of Paul, we are heirs of God, co-heirs with Christ, the Holy Spirit being the present guarantee of that which is to come (Rom. 8:15–17). Or as Hebrews pictures it, we are children of the pilgrims Abraham and Sarah, who looked beyond the land "to the city that has foundations, whose architect and builder is God" (11:10).

The preachers among us need to remember how important it is now and then to take the congregation by the hand and let them walk the boundaries of their inheritance. This promise is kept in place and made new every morning by the watchful power of God that the church continually appropriates by trust. The triumph of God's power will be in the final and complete unveiling of the salvation in which we will participate. Note that this salvation, this completion of God's plan to make creation whole and healthy (the basic meaning of "salvation") and implied in the terms "reconciliation" and "restoration," is "revealed" at the end time. This implies what 1 Peter will say repeatedly, that in the foreknowledge and purpose of God this final triumph of mercy and love is a "done deal," an event not subject to chance or human error.

But in the meantime, how is it back at the church? Verses 6–7 touch on two present conditions and on one which may or may not be an experienced reality for the church. First, believers certainly rejoice in the prospect presented in verses 3–5. Second, this joy is not without bombarding forces against it. The church is enduring a number of trials or tests of its faith. What these are will become more clear to us later in the epistle, but as stated in the introduction, the trials are not in court and martyrdom is not yet in the picture. Most likely social rejection and verbal abuse by prejudiced and hostile neighbors constitute the tests being endured. It is the same old story repeated in new forms of hatred. As these words are being written, "ethnic cleansing" is raging in Bosnia. What is the difference except in intensity? President François Mitterand of France has said that the primary social problem in his country is xenophobia, fear of the stranger, rejection of the outsider, the one who is different. In 1 Peter, Christians are the different ones, the recipients of abuse. Sad to say, but lest we feel self-righteous, remember that in other times and places, Christians have carried the posters, done the screaming, administered the abuse. The writer calls on the church to regard these trials as temporary, however, and as capable of good effect. As gold gains purity from the fire that removes the dross, so faith can be refined by adversity and can emerge from the experience with renewed proof of genuineness. As I stated above, we do not know if we are here dealing with an experienced reality for these Christians. This is to say, we do not know if all or any of the original readers were able or willing to interpret their suffering this way. Today some do and some do not. Suffering in and of itself is not redemptive; suffering has to be interpreted, and that is difficult. We enlist others to help us because uninterpreted pain is the most unbearable, but not all interpretations are equally helpful. This letter will offer a number of understandings of the sufferings of Christians. In these two verses, the message is that those who see their trials as having a clarifying and purifying effect are already joining the chorus of praise that will rise as one grand doxology at the appearing of Jesus Christ.

At the revealing (apocalypse) of Christ, which is the central event of the close of the age, the Christians of Asia Minor will see him for the first time. Unlike the writer who describes himself as a witness of Christ's suffering, these believers are separated by time and distance from the life and death of Jesus. Their love and faith are no less genuine (vv. 8–9) and are to be rewarded no less than that of disciples who knew him during his lifetime. Their faith and ours has been generated by "those who brought you good news by the Holy Spirit" (v. 12); that is, by the preaching of the word. As the risen Christ said to his disciple Thomas: "Have you believed because you have seen me? Blessed are those who have not seen and yet have come to believe" (John 20:29).

The blessing comes to a close (vv. 10–12) with a most unusual statement regarding the continuity between the Old Testament and the New, an affirmation of the single purpose of God throughout the history of God's people. That the writer joins rather than separates the two testaments is to be welcomed because from ancient times to the present too many Christians reject, avoid, or minimally value the Old Testament. Among New Testament writers who affirm the continuity of Old and New Testaments, methods differ and those methods are not all equally impressive. For example, the pattern of promise-fulfillment is widely used, but this should not be interpreted to mean the Old Testament loses its own message and value to the times and circumstances of the later writers. Israel's exodus and desert wanderings were vitally important events in themselves, but they also provide for Christians significant ways to understand their lives as well. When Isaiah said "And a virgin shall conceive, and bear a son" (7:14, KJV), he gave a sign to the king of his day. However, when Christians re-read the Old Testament, they heard in this passage a prophecy of Christ's birth. The one interpretation does not void the other. It is not necessary to make raids on Judaism's scriptures, robbing them of all meaning except our meaning.

However, some who re-read the Old Testament with Christian eyes were not content to find a new and relevant message but pressed to the point of saying that the ancient writers were not even addressing their own generation but were addressing Christians to come centuries later. Here in verses 10–12 the author says the prophets of Israel were earnestly seeking and inquiring after the gospel, the word of grace now embraced by Christians, and the foundation of that good news, the passion and resurrected glory of Christ. To say that the prophets "were serving not themselves but you" (v. 12) is far different from saying that Christians have found in their words meanings about which the prophets, in serving their own people, were unaware at the time. It is one thing to say an Old Testament writer addressed his own generation in ways that spoke anew to Christians later, and quite another to say the writer spoke over the heads of his contemporaries to address persons in a far distant future. These words from 1 Peter push the modern reader to think through this most vital issue because it is not purely academic; Jewish-Christian relationships are implied and imbedded here, as well as how one reads both testaments.

In praise of God's gracious act toward us, the writer not only elevates the gospel as the subject matter of both Jewish prophets and Christian preachers, but he even says angels were interested as well. They wanted to peek into this mystery that God was offering, not to them (Heb. 2:16), but to human beings. There is no implication here that angels were jealous and attempting to thwart the purpose of God, although interfering angels are a theme in some Jewish and Christian writers. This blessing or eulogy ends on a more positive note: angels who rejoice over one sinner who repents (Luke 15:10) are amazed, as we are, at the bounteous grace of God.

CHRISTIANS AS THE HOUSEHOLD OF GOD
1 Peter 1:13–2:10

It is now important to locate the newborn within the household of God. Christians are not isolated children abandoned to the streets to fend for themselves. That they are not orphaned or alone was implied in the word "inheritance" (v. 4), but now more explicitly the readers are placed with a new Father and among brothers and sisters.

As Children with a New Father (1 Peter 1:13–21)

1:13 **Therefore prepare your minds for action; discipline yourselves; set all your hope on the grace that Jesus Christ will bring you when he is revealed.** 14 **Like obedient children, do not be conformed to the desires that you formerly had in ignorance.** 15 **Instead, as he who called you is holy, be holy yourselves in all your conduct,** 16 **for it is written, "You shall be holy, for I am holy."**

17 **If you invoke as Father the one who judges all people impartially according to their deeds, live in reverent fear during the time of your exile.** 18 **You know that you were ransomed from the futile ways inherited from your ancestors, not with perishable things like silver or gold;** 19 **but with the precious blood of Christ, like that of a lamb without defect or blemish.** 20 **He was destined before the foundation of the world, but was revealed at the**

end of the ages for your sake. [21] **Through him you have come to trust in God, who raised him from the dead and gave him glory, so that your faith and hope are set on God.**

After the readers luxuriate in the blessing of verses 3–12, verse 13 comes as a jolt. Given the demands of the Christian life and the pressures of an unfriendly environment, these new Christians will have to grow up fast. "Prepare your minds for action," or literally, "gird up the loins of your minds." Prepare for the life of the exile, the resident alien. The image is that of a person beginning a journey on foot by gathering up at the waist the loose flowing garments. Today we say, "Make up your mind" or "Roll up your sleeves" or "Pull yourself together." The author of Hebrews says, "Lay aside every weight and the sin that clings so closely" (12:1). Discipleship calls for discipline, a word that here in verse 13 means literally "staying completely sober." In religious literature of that day, persons too enamored with the immediate pleasures of life were said to be drunk, asleep, and ignorant of higher values. Hence the New Testament's frequent calls for sobriety, being awake, and turning from a life of ignorance. All the base appetites of their prebaptismal life are to be abandoned in a 180-degree turn toward Christ and the hope presented earlier in the blessing (v. 3). As we shall notice soon, this is not a call to cut themselves off in irresponsible distance from their social and political context. Rather they are to be governed by a new consideration—to live in ways consonant with the character of God. In this sense they are to be holy (vv. 15–16), that is, set apart (Lev. 11:44–45). And what is to be holy? Is it to walk through the world unaware of it, unmoved by it? No; the God who is holy loves the world and provides for it. But God's people are not seduced into confusing Creator and creation. To worship a creation, whatever it is, is to be drunk, asleep, and ignorant. The believer loves as God loves. For example, when Jesus called on his followers to behave as children of the Father in heaven, he focused on the matter of impartiality. Just as God sends sun and rain on the evil and the good, so are we to respond in love to all, not distinguishing between neighbors and foes, friendly and unfriendly, kin and strangers (Matt. 5:43–48). In other words, we are not to be intimidated by nor wrongly attracted to the word "holy." How has God behaved toward us? That is what it means to be holy in all our relationships.

If, then, we are to pattern our conduct on the character of God, it is appropriate to pause in the presentation of the moral imperatives of the Christian life in order to reflect on the nature of this God with whom these new believers have a new relationship. This is the theme of verses

17–21. The recipients of the letter are apparently Gentile in background (v. 14 speaks of their "ignorance," v. 18 of "futile ways inherited from your ancestors"). Had they been Jewish, the writer could have assumed a belief in God that needed only to be informed by God's act in Jesus Christ. As it is, the subject is God on whom their faith and hope are set. Much of the early teaching and preaching of the church was to Jewish audiences who needed to hear not about God but about Jesus as God's Messiah. Regrettably, however, even after the church moved on to address Gentiles, its messages continued to be about Christ to the neglect of the subject of God. The author of 1 Peter makes no such mistake, asserting that it was God who raised Jesus from the dead and that it was through Jesus that they had come to trust in God (v. 21).

Since the subject of God is inexhaustible and every writer or speaker must be selective in treating the matter, what does the writer here choose to say about God to these new Christians? First, he says that as children of God they can call on God as father. Our familiarity with the title should not dull our appreciation for this relationship. God is so addressed in the Old Testament although infrequently (Psalm 89:26; Isa. 63:16; 64:8). Jesus not only called God father (Matt. 7:11; 23:9) but instructed his followers to do so (Matt. 6:9). For Paul, calling on God as father was one of the extraordinary benefits of the Christian life; in Rom. 8:15–16, he wrote, "When we cry, 'Abba! Father!' it is that very Spirit bearing witness with our spirit that we are children of God." Before the father, the children live in "reverent fear" (v. 17), or as we express it in the Lord's Prayer, "hallowed be your name."

Second, the writer portrays God as judge. This may seem strange to us who may not ordinarily put father and judge in the same sentence. However, the Bible knows what we sometimes forget, and that is: Judgment is not a contradiction of love but rather a function of love. Judging need not mean condemning or criticizing; it does mean distinguishing right from wrong, holding up a standard with expectation that it be observed. An absence of moral and ethical demands would hardly be a demonstration of a parent's love for children. It may have been that the readers' background was such that they did not associate religion and morality as does both Judaism and Christianity. And just in case the word "father" sounded a bit soft and permissive, the instruction here is appropriate for the newly baptized. That God judges without partiality on the basis of one's works (v. 17; also Acts 10:34; Rom. 2:11) is both good news to those who may worry that God operates with a double standard and a firm reminder to those who may assume they are insiders and therefore measured by a different scale. On the contrary, judgment will actually begin with the household of God (4:17).

Third, the author of 1 Peter notes that God has ransomed us (v. 18). This metaphor of redemption has roots in the Old Testament image of buying freedom from slavery (Isa. 52:3) and came to be a widely used term among Christians to refer to being set free from sin (Mark 10:45; 1 Cor. 6:20; Titus 2:14). The ransom price was extremely high; no amount of gold or silver would achieve it (vv. 18–19). Rather the cost was the sacrifice of Christ, here portrayed in the imagery of the lamb slain for sin (Heb. 9:12, 14; Rev. 5:9). According to the ancient practice of Israel, such lambs had to be carefully selected, for only one completely free of defect was acceptable. The writer is quick to point out, however, that Jesus was not a victim, as a lamb might be. He was not caught and put to death in some scheme to hinder the plan of God. To be sure, those who killed Jesus thought they were the ones with power of life and death, and for his death they are accountable. But our author understands that God, who can turn human wrath into praise, had a purpose that extended from the foundation of the world to these last days (v. 20) and that purpose was to ransom us from sin through Christ. In this sense Christ was slain from the foundation of the world, and such an understanding is possible by means of God's revelation, which has come now at the end of the ages (Rom. 16:25–27).

We need to pause a moment here to reflect on the conversion of those "ransomed." Their former life is only vaguely described as "the futile ways inherited from your ancestors" (v. 18). That they were Gentiles is clear, but what kind? It is easy and popular to portray them in the worst possible light because conversions are more dramatic and seem to honor the power of the gospel if the gulf between "formerly" and "but now" is extremely wide. The diamond of the new life shines brighter against a dark background. Of course, there were also, as there are now, persons converted from very respectable lives. Among the Greeks were moral philosophers and teachers who condemned the gross and irresponsible behavior of "the thoughtless." We do not know the pasts of these Christians of Asia Minor, and our not knowing should restrain imagination and speculation rather than release it.

Finally, this God who is to the church father, judge, and redeemer is the one who has wooed our trust and hope through the death and resurrection of Christ. We spoke of this earlier in this section, but it remains to be said that the life of Jesus Christ has revealed the nature of God, showing us that we can confidently put our trust and hope in God. As Paul said, "There are many gods and many lords" (1 Cor. 8:5), and to believe in one or more of them is not necessarily liberating. In Jesus Christ we have an answer to the question put to the early missionaries: What kind of God is this one of whom you speak? Looking to Jesus, they could say that whoever has seen him has seen God (John 14:9).

This understanding of God is all the more life-giving to those who are described as being in "the time of your exile" (v. 17). It is not fully clear whether exile is to be understood as being away from their heavenly home (Phil. 3:20; Heb. 13:14) or as being strangers and outsiders socially. Perhaps both. It is worth noting that the word translated as "exile" here is different from the word similarly translated in 1:1. In 1:1 the readers are addressed as strangers, transients moving through the land. In 1:17 the word refers to residents who are in another's land and therefore without the civil rights of natives. Perhaps the most moving account of such a life is to be found in the Wisdom of Ben Sirach 29:21–28.

> The necessities of life are water, bread, and clothing,
>   and also a house to assure privacy.
> Better is the life of the poor under their own crude roof
>   than sumptuous food in the house of others.
> Be content with little or much,
>   and you will hear no reproach for being a guest.
> It is a miserable life to go from house to house;
>   as a guest you should not open your mouth;
> you will play the host and provide drink without being thanked,
>   and besides this you will hear rude words like these:
> "Come here, stranger, prepare the table;
>   let me eat what you have there."
> "Be off, stranger, for an honored guest is here;
>   my brother has come for a visit, and I need the guest-room."
> It is hard for a sensible person to bear
>   scolding about lodging and the insults of the moneylender.

In Acts 13:17 the word here translated "exile" is rendered "stay," referring to Israel's stay in the land of Egypt. In later Christian writers such as Polycarp, Clement, and Irenaeus, the word occurs as a synonym for "church." When the Greek word is transliterated into English, it is "parochial," meaning to be at home only within the parish, not the larger community. Perhaps a look at the original word may be helpful: it is *paroikos*. Since the word for household is *oikos*, the two words alone (*par* means "beside" but not "inside") capture the tension in which the Christians live. They are members of the *oikos* of God but their present social and cultural experience is that of the *paroikos*, the exile, the outsider, the one without a home. A major burden of this letter is to assure the readers that even as exiles they most certainly live within the household of God.

As Children with New Brothers and Sisters
(1 Peter 1:22–2:3)

1:22 **Now that you have purified your souls by your obedience to the truth so that you have genuine mutual love, love one another deeply from the heart.** 23 **You have been born anew, not of perishable but of imperishable seed, through the living and enduring word of God.** 24 **For**
  "All flesh is like grass
       and all its glory like the flower of grass.
  The grass withers,
       and the flower falls,
    25 **but the word of the Lord endures forever."**
That word is the good news that was announced to you.

2:1 **Rid yourselves, therefore, of all malice, and all guile, insincerity, envy, and all slander.** 2 **Like newborn infants, long for the pure, spiritual milk, so that by it you may grow into salvation—**3 **if indeed you have tasted that the Lord is good.**

Verses 13–21 set the Christian before God as father, with appropriate reminders of the imperatives that are implied in that relationship. Now the writer sets the Christian among the new brothers and sisters who come with God as father. The recipients are not allowed to assume this new faith of theirs is simply a "God and I" relationship. To be in the household of God is to be in an extended family. The word "extended" is important here because the nuclear family, for all its pleasures and stability, does not serve well as an image of the church. To say "ours is a family church" sounds warm and cozy, but such churches, of whatever size, can be exclusive if "family" means we look alike, sound alike, eat alike, vote alike, socialize alike, and are resistant to diversity. An extended family has to work at its relationships constantly because even a person with the most sincere faith in the grace of God must still deal with the social, economic, and ethnic barriers that are in the culture and that do not automatically collapse like the walls of Jericho the day after baptism. It is one of the popular fictions of religious culture that once "the heart is right" all other obstacles to Christian living disappear. Not so. Even the most thoroughly converted persons have to work at it. But the benefits that come from these new brother-and-sister relationships are so mutually sustaining and life-giving that one wonders how anyone could presume to be a Christian alone. But the writer of 1 Peter knows that the background of the readers has not prepared them for the most extraordinary piece of Christian furniture, the pew, which invites former strangers to sit together as a family. And being new Christians, their need for guidance and instruction is all the more urgent.

In 1:22–2:3, therefore, the readers of 1 Peter are given two images of their apparently recent conversion—the "purified soul," and being "born anew." Each image is accompanied by instruction in Christian relationships that the image implies. The first image is that of the purified soul (v. 22). The reference to purification is reminiscent of ritual cleansing of cooking utensils, clothing, foods, and, of course, the human body. Perhaps the writer again has baptism in mind, but the notion of ritual cleansing is joined to moral cleansing: "you have purified your souls" (see also James 4:8; 1 John 3:3). And moral cleansing does not come by ritual alone but "by your obedience to the truth." The writer has already spoken of "obedient children" and "discipline" (vv. 13–14), joining an array of New Testament writers (for example, Acts 6:7; Rom. 1:5) who are not afraid of these words. But words like "obedience" seem increasingly foreign to modern ears, and somewhat grating. Biblically the word comes from the verb "to hear" in the sense of "sitting under" a word and submitting ourselves to its claim on us. In scripture, listening, truly listening, is already obedience, in the Bible's conviction that to hear the word of God is to be affected by it, to be changed by it. Disobedience is a refusal to listen, primarily because we know that if we listen our lives may be altered. I have often reminded students in preaching classes that it is not only poor preaching to which people refuse to listen; it is to good preaching as well. The word makes its claim on those who hear.

Immediately the author states the purpose of purifying the soul: "so that you have genuine mutual love" (v. 22). Note: purifying their souls is not a form of spiritual self-indulgence but has a social aim, mutual love (literally, *philadelphia*, "love of brothers and sisters"). This love is genuine; that is, not hypocritical, not a pretense, not a stage act. And it is already theirs. In other words, love of these new brothers and sisters is a given of their conversion, an affirmation not an imperative. With the new life one is given new relationships and the capacity to be at home in the new family. Then strikingly the affirmation becomes an injunction: "love one another deeply from the heart" (v. 22). In other words, you are brothers and sisters, so act like it. You have the gift of love, so express it. Christians are instructed to become the family that they are. The language and the sentiment recall Paul's admonition: "Let love be genuine; hate what is evil, hold fast to what is good; love one another with mutual affection; outdo one another in showing honor" (Rom. 12:9–10). The ways in which love shows itself are determined by an alertness and sensitivity to one another's needs.

The second image for conversion is that of being born anew (v. 23). This expression, especially appropriate for the newly baptized, has been used earlier (v. 3), but here it is joined to the agent of the new birth, the word of God. The word of God refers in this case specifically to "the good news that was announced to you" (v. 25; also v. 12). Saying that the preaching of the gospel is powerful is not a way of complimenting the abilities of those who came preaching in Asia Minor but is rather a continuation of the entire Bible's conviction that a word is powerful, and especially God's word. Creation, judgment, regeneration, and revelation follow the simple expression "And God said." And in a similar way, our words can do and undo. By a word the weary are sustained (Isa. 50:4), but by a word one can crush and inflict pain. In fact, Jesus said, "By your words you will be justified, and by your words you will be condemned" (Matt. 12:37).

It is no contradiction of this power to call the word of God a seed. Jesus did so quite often (see the parables in Mark 4). It is fragile, to be sure: birds can carry it away and weeds can choke it (Mark 4:3–8). After all, is not preaching the creation of vibrating air against an eardrum? And yet that word creates new life and new communities such as those addressed in 1 Peter and those to which we belong. The word of God that generates and sustains the family of faith can be opposed, ridiculed, and rejected, but it endures forever. To help celebrate that conviction the writer quotes Isa. 40:6–8.

Of all the qualities of the word of God that could be extolled, the one underlined here is its imperishability. How appropriate this focus is for a minority living as resident aliens in an unfriendly society! In fact, already the readers have repeatedly had the assurance of permanence. Reflect on the verses we have read thus far: destined; an inheritance that is imperishable; unfading; kept in heaven; protected by the power of God; unlike perishable gold or silver; before the foundation of the world. But believers do not have to be abused, isolated, and persecuted to hear good and welcome news in these words. The changing of the seasons, the endless need for repair to our homes, the increased frequency of trips to the physician, the loss of relatives and friends, the moving away of good neighbors, the growing realization that no amount of savings can guarantee a comfortable future—these and countless other reminders of the transient nature of life prompt us to cling to promising words such as these: "The grass withers, and the flower falls, but the word of the Lord endures forever" (vv. 24–25, quoting Isa. 40:8).

Just as the first image, purified souls, carried with it an admonition to love the brothers and sisters, so the second image, new birth, prompts its own moral instruction (2:1–3). It is natural to follow through on the metaphor of birth to speak of the newly baptized as infants who need pure milk in order to grow. To distinguish between beginning and later instruction in Christian living, the analogies of milk and meat (solid food) seem to have been widely used (1 Cor. 3:2; Heb. 5:12–14). In some churches of the second century, milk and honey were fed to initiates after baptism. This analogy of taking nourishment prompts the writer to draw on Psalm 34:8: "O taste and see that the LORD is good!"

Christian growth involves, among other things, getting rid of those attitudes, ways of speaking, and behavior patterns that attack the central fabric of the community: mutual love. It is naive to think these erosive forces are permanently washed away at baptism, and it is an impossible burden to place on any program of Christian education to expect that it will exterminate these evils entirely. To be able to assume that qualities destructive of the fellowship are found only among those still wet from baptism and that in time they will grow out of such disruptive behavior would indeed be encouraging, but long experience points to the contrary. Malice, envy, and slander do not drop off like old clothes; these demons must be fought to the end. In fact, just when one thinks they have been exorcised, the spiritual life is at its greatest peril (Luke 11:24–26).

There is no reason for us to think that the author's list of diseases in the churches of Asia Minor—malice, deceit, insincerity, envy, and slander—is shaped to address problems peculiar to any one congregation. No matter to how many congregations the letter circulated nor how many have read the letter since that time, the list is both general enough and specific enough to speak to all. Yet we continue to be both surprised and embarrassed that this is true. Perhaps it is because members of a community, no matter how close knit, never completely mature. Maybe it is because religion sometimes brings out the worst as well as the best in us. Our faith and its attendant values are so deeply important to us that even hints of change or threat to those convictions can be incendiary. It is certainly the case that in an atmosphere of mutual love and trust we are most vulnerable and, therefore, getting rid of pain-inflicting speech and behavior is always in every church an urgent business. But even persons who love each

other cause pain by inattention, thoughtlessness, and ignorance. Therefore, the survival of the church always has depended and will continue to
depend on a constant climate of forgiveness, spoken and unspoken.

Forming a New Temple of God (1 Peter 2:4–10)

2:4 **Come to him, a living stone, though rejected by mortals yet chosen and
precious in God's sight, and** [5] **like living stones, let yourselves be built into
a spiritual house, to be a holy priesthood, to offer spiritual sacrifices acceptable to God through Jesus Christ.** [6] **For it stands in scripture:**

"See, I am laying in Zion a stone,
a cornerstone chosen and precious;
and whoever believes in him will not be put to shame."

[7] **To you then who believe, he is precious: but for those who do not believe,**

"The stone that the builders rejected
has become the very head of the corner,"

[8] **and**

"A stone that makes them stumble,
and a rock that makes them fall."

They stumble because they disobey the word, as they were destined to do.
[9] **But you are a chosen race, a royal priesthood, a holy nation, God's own
people, in order that you may proclaim the mighty acts of him who called
you out of darkness into his marvelous light.**

[10] **Once you were not a people,**
but now you are God's people;
once you had not received mercy,
but now you have received mercy.

The shift from infants to stones seems sudden, and it is. However, two factors soften the jolt. First, the Psalm quoted in verse 3 (34:8) very likely is
still in the writer's mind, for that Psalm twice says "Come to him" (in the
Greek translation of the psalm). Verse 4 thus seems a more natural transition. Secondly, although the image changes, the theme does not.

First Peter 1:22–2:3 dealt with relationships in the church, and so does
the discussion of temple, priesthood, and people of God. The temple is
here not the individual body (as in 1 Cor. 6:19) but the community as a
corporate body (as in 1 Cor. 3:16–17). A fuller expression of this view is
found in Eph. 2:19–22:

"So then you are no longer strangers and aliens, but you are citizens with
the saints and also members of the household of God, built upon the foundation of the apostles and prophets, with Christ Jesus himself as the cor-

nerstone. In him the whole structure is joined together and grows into a holy temple in the Lord; in whom you also are built together spiritually into a dwelling place for God."

Likewise, the expressions "a chosen race, a royal priesthood, a holy nation, God's own people" (v. 9) are clearly community and not individual designations. We have not, then, in this unit shifted from the principal accent of the passage immediately preceding.

The image of Christ as a living stone and Christians as living stones dominates this passage. If the word "living" seems awkward in relation to a stone, remember the writer is very aware of his and the readers' religious world in which "dead" stone idols abounded. As for the stone imagery, it was already quite popular in both Jewish and Christian teaching about God, Israel, Messiah, and church. Verses 6–8 consist almost entirely of Old Testament citations (Isa. 28:16; Psalm 118:22; Isa. 8:14–15) that very likely had been joined as stone sayings useful for teaching prior to 1 Peter. The Dead Sea Scrolls show their use by the community at Qumran, and the New Testament contains ample evidence of Christian preachers employing them, including Jesus himself (Matt. 21:42; Acts 4:11).

The imagery is mixed, and so for the sake of clarity we will separate the three ideas imbedded here: Christ the stone, Christians as stones, and Christians as a priesthood. As for Christ the stone, early Christians used the three texts cited as prophecies of God's act in Jesus Christ. The first (Isa. 28:16) is a broad affirmation of God's initiating act of grace. God has provided in Christ a firm and certain foundation for faith, and those who trust God's act will find that sufficient. There will be no reason for shame or disgrace. The ground of faith is fully adequate.

The second (Psalm 118:22) was taken as a prophecy of the death and resurrection of Christ. The picture is that of a construction crew engaged in building a house or temple. They toss aside one stone that they regard as having no place according to their blueprints. But the very stone they reject (crucifixion) God the master builder places as the keystone or capstone in the arch (resurrection) that completes the structure. What human beings want to build and what God is building are not always the same. But God is God, and the rejections or refusals among us do not finally defeat the plan of God.

The third and final citation (Isa. 8:14–15) is about a stone that may help or hinder, an aid for stepping or a cause for stumbling. Isaiah said God may be a sanctuary or a stone one strikes against. This citation was much used in the church's attempt to understand the rejection of Christ by many of his own as well as by subsequent generations. If God places a stone on the path and some find it helpful for their journey while others stumble, did God cause both the stepping and the stumbling? It is easy enough to classify some as believing and obedient and others as disbelieving and disobedient, and so they are. And it is even easier to praise God for the believers and blame the disbelievers for their own stumbling. But the scriptures, which insist that all things have their beginning and end in God, attribute to God both the blessing and the bane, both the stepping and the stumbling. The stone God places before them makes them stumble. God creates both light and darkness, or as Simeon said of the Christ, "This child is destined for the falling and the rising of many in Israel" (Luke 2:34). Paul wrestled with this problem as he agonized over Israel's rejection of Christ (Romans 9). Did God intend such rejection? Paul's resolution came with the insight that Israel's temporary rejection of Christ would work for the opening of the opportunity for faith to Gentiles, and that finally God's purpose to include all, both Jew and Greek, would be fulfilled (Romans 10—11). However one wrestles with the tension between God's will and human freedom, the love of God that desires that none should perish but that all should come to faith should never be left outside the discussion. Even so, everyone who seeks to make a difference in the world cannot avoid the pain that is God's pain: In the very act of trying to help, have my efforts hindered some? Every well-meaning parent ponders this matter in the rearing of children. Every preacher feels the pain of it when someone leaves angrily during the preaching of good news. Did I drive someone farther away? Did I place a stumbling stone in the path? Whoever walks into a room and turns on a light has thereby created shadows, but what is the alternative?

Christians may be spoken of as living stones because they are changed into Christ's own image (2 Cor. 3:18). Christ and his people are one (John 17:21–23). As already noted, this image of believers as stones forming the house of God became widely used (1 Cor. 3:16–17; Eph. 2:20–22) with multiple meanings. For example, the community became the dwelling place of the Spirit as God had dwelt as a cloud of glory in the Temple Holy of Holies. The image also served in exhortations to unity within the church. Later, in a Christian writing called *The Shepherd of Hermas*, the stone image was developed into an extended allegory with strong moral instruction. Much attention was given to describing stones that fit and stones that did not fit and hence were tossed aside. This portrayal of Christians as stones joined together also extends the admonition to mutual love in 1:22. Hear a parable: A certain person decided to build a church. To insure strength and durability, the builder carefully selected stones exactly alike: same size, shape, and color. They were put in place with pride and confidence, but when the wind blew and the storm rose, the church was destroyed. Another builder decided to construct a church. Stones of different sizes, shapes, and colors were gathered. How could such a church survive? Strong cement was mixed and applied between the stones. When the wind blew and the storm rose, the church stood firm. Such is the power of mutual love.

The third image is that of Christians as priests (v. 5). Since the Protestant Reformation many Christians have understood the priesthood of believers primarily in two ways: the freedom of individuals to approach God without an intermediary other than Christ, and the obligation to pray for each other and serve one another's needs. These are important understandings, but in our text "priesthood" refers to the community of believers, not to individuals. How does a community "offer spiritual sacrifices"? The writer does not elaborate, and so we may ask others in the New Testament how they understood the priesthood of the church. The author of Hebrews speaks primarily of the church at worship. "Through him, then, let us continually offer a sacrifice of praise to God, that is, the fruit of lips that confess his name" (13:15). But interestingly, the writer continues with the language of worship in another vein. "Do not neglect to do good and to share what you have, for such sacrifices are pleasing to God" (13:16). In other words, both voice and deeds constitute proper praise. Nothing in 1 Peter would sever the two. Rather than being anti-ritual as some have claimed, the writer presses ritual to include relationships and benevolent behavior. Paul, likewise, wrote of the Christian life as worship: "Present your bodies as a living sacrifice, holy and acceptable to God, which is your spiritual worship" (Rom. 12:1). In addition, he regarded ministry, and in particular missionary work, as worship. "Because of the grace given me by God to be a minister of Christ Jesus to the Gentiles in the priestly service of the gospel of God, so that the offering of the Gentiles may be acceptable, sanctified by the Holy Spirit" (Rom. 15:15–16). It would be safe to say that if these elaborations of the image of priesthood—acts of praise, deeds of kindness, sharing of goods, acceptable conduct, and proclamation of the gospel—were brought to 1 Peter 2:5, the writer would say, "Amen." And no doubt the God in whose priestly service we are would say, "Yes."

This unit concludes (vv. 9–10) with two powerful affirmations of the Christian community, affirmations all the more striking because they are addressed to Gentile Christians. Both statements originally referred to

Jews, to Israel, who had been chosen to be a light to the nations and to testify to the gracious activity of the God who called them out of darkness into God's light. Christians, even Gentile Christians, lay claim to both the affirmation and the mission. This does not mean Israel has been rejected but that Gentiles have been included. After all, as Paul would say it, Abraham and Sarah are the forebears of all who believe, both Jew and Gentile (Romans 4). The first affirmation draws on Exod. 19:6, God's word to Moses that was to be spoken to the people. Israel, like the church, was just beginning to be formed and its identity established. Thus Moses said to Israel, as 1 Peter 2:9 says to its readers then and now, you are God's people because God has chosen you. You are, therefore, to be holy as God is holy, and your unceasing work is to offer to God appropriate praise and sacrifice.

The second affirmation quotes Hos. 2:23. The prophet Hosea was married to Gomer who became unfaithful and left him for a foreign lover. She later returned in penitent tears, and he accepted her. Hosea had, therefore, lived out in his marriage and family the adulterous departure of Israel from God to idols and God's forgiveness upon Israel's return. Under divine mandate, Hosea named a daughter "Not pitied" (Lo-ruhamah) and a son "Not my people" (Lo-ammi). But by God's gracious redemption of Israel, "Not pitied" became "Pitied" and "Not my people" became "My people." With these words the church remembers its former life and its present identity. These terms of sharp contrast—"once you were" but "now you are"—are often referred to as the language of conversion, and so it is. But it is also the language of confession appropriate for every gathering of the church, not in dramatic beating of the breast but in sincere gratitude and praise. The community of faith looks around at itself and says, "This is the Lord's doing, and it is marvelous in our eyes."

CHRISTIANS AS ALIENS IN THE WORLD
1 Peter 2:11–3:12

Thus far the letter has asked the reader to think about life before God and among brothers and sisters of like faith. In other words, the conversation has been family talk and any tensions addressed were intramural only. Now the time has come to move outside and consider the larger social and political context. That context is a world the readers know all too well, having only recently turned from it to a new life in Christ. Is it possible to look on the old life with new eyes, to view the once familiar as now strange? Granted the debauchery of the former life is unquestionably to be laid aside, but is nothing from the past to be salvaged? If discriminating judgments are to be made about prebaptism associations and activities, what are the criteria? The original readers are learning what we are learning: It is difficult to be in but not of the world. On a recent plane trip, the passenger in the next seat noticed my reading material and asked, "Are you a Christian?" When I said, "Yes," she asked further, "Do you mean by that that you are not Moslem or Jew, or do you mean it in a personal and intentional way?" I replied that I was by faith and commitment a Christian, and wondered aloud why she asked. "Until recently," she said, "I was generally classified as a Christian, but now widowed with two teenagers to raise in a world of violence, drugs, and permissiveness, I have had to put up or shut up. But being sincere is not enough. Decisions are tough, and I need help." For two hours we tried to help each other. It is to that need the writer of 1 Peter now turns.

Aliens Both Transient and Resident (1 Peter 2:11–12)

2:11 Beloved, I urge you as aliens and exiles to abstain from the desires of the flesh that wage war against the soul. 12 Conduct yourselves honorably among the Gentiles, so that, though they malign you as evildoers, they may see your honorable deeds and glorify God when he comes to judge.

These two verses serve both as transition to new subject matter and as introduction to the fundamental posture of the church in that culture. Unless the Christians move into a lonely desert or a high-walled compound, life has to continue for them at the same address. This means matters of employment, entertainment, education of children, dress, food, recreation, and political responsibility must be addressed. Basic to all that follows, says the writer, is your status as "aliens and exiles." The two words have appeared earlier, in 1:1 and 1:17, at which points they were discussed. Joining them here not only follows an ancient precedent (Gen. 23:4; Psalm 39:12 in the Greek version) but serves to underscore an important self-understanding. This identity as aliens and exiles is formed from two ingredients: the way the Christians view themselves and the way society perceives them. The two are not unrelated, as the writer will show.

The place to begin, says verse 11, is with one's own integrity. Interestingly, this is also the beginning point for James (4:1). That all have inner struggles is a common acknowledgment. Jewish theology called it the battle between two spirits within us, the spirit of good and the spirit of evil.

Paul referred to it sometimes as flesh versus spirit (Gal. 5:16–17) and sometimes the law of God versus the law in one's members (Rom. 7:22–23). Our text sees the struggle as between flesh and soul. Two cautions are in order: One, "flesh" in such contexts is not the equivalent of "body," as though the physical body were by its nature evil and a source of evil. Not so. The body is God's creation, and forms of spirituality that deny or seek to escape the body contradict both creation and incarnation; that is, God has come to us in a physical body, Jesus of Nazareth. While the human body is sometimes referred to as the flesh in a physical sense, in the ethical vocabulary of the New Testament, including 1 Peter 2:11, "flesh" refers to the human ego in pursuit of gratification and in that pursuit placing greater value on created things than on the Creator. This indulgence may be of the body, the mind, or even of the spirit. To regard one's own pleasures as primary, whatever they are and whether or not they are socially or even religiously approved, is to live according to the flesh. The spirit or soul seeks the mind of God and the good of others.

The second caution is that the search for integrity, the conquest of the desires of the flesh, is not an end in itself. One could spend a lifetime tinkering with one's soul—more time alone, more retreats, more self-judgment, more self-improvement, more searching for one's center—and at the end have no record of self-denial in the quest for the other's good, no risky investment in altering the oppressive conditions under which others live, no voice raised in the public forum of conflicting values. Religious self-centeredness is seeking to save one's life and that, even if it is called spirituality, is finally fatal. Recall Jesus' recital of the final judgment (Matt. 25:31–46). Those who are invited to spend eternity in the joy of the Lord are totally surprised. Such are the saints: They are self-forgetful.

Perhaps for this reason the author of our text moves quickly to matters social and political. The call is for conduct that, even in the face of verbal abuse, is so favorably impressive that one's attackers will praise God on the day of God's visitation (the NRSV translates as "when he comes to judge" a word that refers to official oversight or superintending, often translated "being a bishop"). This is to say, let your life among your neighbors and in the community be such as to turn their minds toward the God who inspires and informs your behavior. This is a difficulty of some magnitude. We know the source of this instruction: "Let your light shine before others, so that they may see your good works and give glory to your Father in heaven" (Matt. 5:16), but that makes its implementation no easier. What is demanded is not simply good works but such activity carried out in a manner and with an attitude that prompts the critical observer to

praise not the doer but God. Some think that to expect evangelistic effectiveness from Christian conduct is naive. Perhaps so, but Christian history
bears many examples of the persuasiveness of the benevolent and forgiving life, just as it does of the failure of the witness of churches that are sat-
isfied with self-serving programs.

We cannot know exactly what is involved in doing honorable (good)
works and as a result being maligned for doing evil works (v. 12). It could
be simply explained as another case of misinterpreting every act and word
of those who are hated or viewed with suspicion. Or perhaps we have a
case of guilt by misidentification. There were many religious groups in
Asia Minor, some of which were politically subversive. For example, "benefit clubs" were organizations of poor people who banded together to help
each other, but on occasion civil disobedience and violence against local
governments erupted. Some other cults, such as the Bacchae, held noc-
turnal orgies in worshiping the god of pleasure. Quite possibly local citizens heard of the Christian groups and concluded, "Another one of those
troublesome religions." We do know that there were charges that Christians met secretly and practiced incest and cannibalism, accusations most
likely stemming from distorted interpretations of love feasts and the Eucharist. Even so, we must not idealize the early church. At the beginning
of the second century, the governor of Bithynia and Pontus, when inves-
tigating "Christian clubs," found more who admitted to once having been
Christian than he did those who were presently committed to the faith.
And most likely, then as now, there were enough in the churches engaged
in unacceptable behavior to bring down criticism on the entire assembly.

Under Authority Yet Free (1 Peter 2:13–17)

2:13 **For the Lord's sake accept the authority of every human institution,
whether of the emperor as supreme,** [14] **or of governors, as sent by him to
punish those who do wrong and to praise those who do right.** [15] **For it is
God's will that by doing right you should silence the ignorance of the foolish.** [16] **As servants of God, live as free people, yet do not use your freedom
as a pretext for evil.** [17] **Honor everyone. Love the family of believers. Fear
God. Honor the emperor.**

It is generally recognized that 2:13–3:7 conforms to a pattern of ethical
instruction found among both Jews and Greeks that is commonly called a
table of household duties. It consisted of brief instructions to wives and
husbands, children and parents, slaves and masters. The Christian church

found the form and some of the content useful, as its appearances in the New Testament testify (Eph. 5:21–6:9; Col. 3:18–4:1; 1 Timothy 2—3; Titus 2:1–10). Both New Testament and subsequent Christian writers modified the instructions in each case, prompted by differing circumstances and judgments as to what was and what was not compatible with the gospel. The first unit of the section deals with the church's relationship to society in general and to the government in particular. By the fact that the passage (vv. 13–17) begins and ends with instruction about the emperor, we can conclude that this was a major concern to the writer. The church has, from the beginning, been concerned to live peacefully in society. Listen to these voices: "All who believed were together. . . . praising God and having the goodwill of all the people" (Acts 2:44, 47). "If it is possible, so far as it depends on you, live peaceably with all" (Rom. 12:18). "Conduct yourselves wisely toward outsiders, making the most of the time" (Col. 4:5). However, the relationship of the Christian community to the government in particular has been and remains a complex issue. There are circumstances in many countries that convert the comfortable "for God *and* country" to the painful "for God *or* country."

At the outset it is only fair to keep in mind that historically not only has religion had problems with governments but governments have had problems with religion. This includes the Roman Empire under which the churches addressed in 1 Peter lived. We could think more clearly on this matter if we could erase from memory old movies and novels that give the impression that from day one, Roman soldiers were crucifying, burning, and tossing to lions all who confessed faith in Christ. Robert Wilken wrote a book that helps clear our vision. Published by Yale University Press in 1984, it is written for the general reader, not the specialist, but is no less thoroughly researched. In *The Christians as the Romans Saw Them*, Wilken reminds us that Rome's general policy, in its effort to keep peace and to avoid insurrection in any of its far-flung provinces, was to respect local traditions and religions. Rome had no desire to interfere with "foolish superstitions." There were, no doubt, breaches in this policy in various provinces, depending on local prejudices and the temperament of magistrates in power. The earliest known record from a non-Christian source of Rome's attitude toward Christians is in the correspondence between the Emperor Trajan and Pliny, his appointed governor for the provinces of Bithynia and Pontus in Asia Minor. Pliny's dates were A.D 111–113, one or possibly two generations later than 1 Peter.

Pliny was sent to Asia Minor to correct a problem of misuse of public funds by local authorities and to investigate the many associations or clubs that had ostensibly noble purposes but may have been politically subversive. It was very popular to belong to one or more of these groups: volunteer firefighters, benevolence societies, park improvement committees, support groups for the elderly, and countless other groups in addition to religious sects. Pliny heard of Christians as one of these "clubs." Some local citizens and merchants complained about the Christians, but the issue is not clear. Perhaps it had to do with the refusal of some believers to purchase meat if it was known to have been sacrificed and dedicated to idols. The emperor instructed Pliny not to hunt down Christians nor to investigate them on the basis of anonymous charges. Trajan was concerned only if the charge was sedition and if it was proven that Christians were not loyal to Rome. Following investigation, Pliny gave Trajan this report about the Christians:

> They declared that the total of their guilt or error amounted to no more than this; they had met regularly before dawn on a fixed day to chant verses alternately among themselves in honor of Christ as if to a god, and also to bind themselves by oath, not for any criminal purpose, but to abstain from theft, robbery, and adultery, to commit no breach of trust and not to deny a deposit when called upon to restore it. After this ceremony it had been their custom to disperse and reassemble later to take food of an ordinary harmless kind (Wilken, 22).

Pliny did, however, find the Christians stubborn and obstinate, and since stubbornness before a Roman official was against the law, he punished them. In fact, he arrived at the conclusion that wearing the name "Christian" was grounds for some kind of punishment even though he expressed grave doubts about there being real danger from "this foolish superstition."

As has already been said, the Pliny-Trajan correspondence is probably a full generation, and possibly two, later than 1 Peter. However, it does provide the thinking of an emperor and a governor from the very same geographical area on the vexing business of what to do with Christians. Neither their correspondence nor 1 Peter reflects an official imperial position against the church, but both reveal tensions between some local citizens and the Christians. Against this background perhaps 1 Peter 2:13–17 will be to us more clear and more real.

We should be cautious about reading into 1 Peter 2:13–17 a reflection of concrete conditions in the provinces in which the churches were located. After all, this is a general epistle circulating over a wide area. Perhaps closer to the truth is the view that the writer is providing general instructions for Christians under Roman authority. It might be instructive to compare our text with two others in the New Testament on the same subject. The one most familiar, perhaps because of its frequent use in Christian assemblies at Thanksgiving and on the Sunday prior to July Fourth, is 1 Tim. 2:1–4:

> First of all, then, I urge that supplications, prayers, intercessions, and thanksgivings be made for everyone, for kings and all who are in high positions, so that we may lead a quiet and peaceable life in all godliness and dignity. This is right and is acceptable in the sight of God our Savior, who desires everyone to be saved and to come to the knowledge of the truth.

This worshipful expression of the church's desire regarding its life among the governments of the world is one with which few would quarrel: pray for all who carry the power and the burden of government so that all of us may live in peace with dignity, to the end that the gospel be unhindered in its embrace of all people everywhere. Such is God's desire.

The second parallel text is Rom. 13:1–7:

> Let every person be subject to the governing authorities: for there is no authority except from God, and those authorities that exist have been instituted by God. Therefore whoever resists authority resists what God has appointed, and those who resist will incur judgment. For rulers are not a terror to good conduct, but to bad. Do you wish to have no fear of the authority? Then do what is good, and you will receive its approval: for it is God's servant for your good. But if you do what is wrong, you should be afraid, for the authority does not bear the sword in vain! It is the servant of God to execute wrath on the wrongdoer. Therefore one must be subject, not only because of wrath but also because of conscience. For the same reason you also pay taxes, for the authorities are God's servants, busy with this very thing. Pay to all what is due them—taxes to whom taxes are due, revenue to whom revenue is due, respect to whom respect is due, honor to whom honor is due.

With this passage 1 Peter shows real kinship. Was there a common source? Perhaps, but it could be argued (and some do) that 1 Peter 2:13–17 is dependent on Romans 13. After all, 1 Peter is from Rome (5:13), which had earlier received Paul's letter to the Christians in that city. However, more striking than the similarities are the differences. Unlike Romans, 1 Peter does not refer to the government as ordained by God nor to the officials as God's servants carrying out God's will. Rather these are human institutions which for God's sake we honor and respect. They are not God's servants; we are. Emperors and governors are to be honored, but only God is to be feared. They are to be honored, but so is everyone. The conduct of the faithful is not out of fear of government but as free service to God with the hoped-for result that critics who do not understand the Christian faith will be sufficiently impressed to be silenced in their attacks. In all their behavior the believers are to be a community of love. No one is to press the principle of Christian freedom to the point of indulging in behavior that hurts the community, dishonors God, and contradicts our identity as God's servants.

Do the differences between Romans 13 and 1 Peter 2 reflect a changed relationship of the government toward the church? Possibly, but even so, 1 Peter can still speak of the governing authorities as punishing those who do wrong and praising those who do right (2:14). Christians could hardly ask for more than that. Conditions have not deteriorated to the level reflected in Revelation, a document also written to Christians in Asia Minor. In that book Christians are alerted to expect from the state persecution and martyrdom. After persecutions of varying extent, duration, and intensity came the state's embrace of the church. Christianity became the official religion of the empire. With that endorsement came subsidies, tax exemptions, large grants of land, clergy in king's houses, official holidays, church membership for everybody, and even the persecuting and outlawing of other religions. To this day, and even in America with its separation of church and state, remnants of Rome's embrace remain.

It is appropriate to ask if we are still instructed by 1 Peter 2:13–17. The answer is, in several ways, yes. First, the early church, though young, very much a minority, and struggling with new issues, faced up to and addressed the matter of its relation to the larger society and to government in particular. It refused to deny that this is God's world by creation and by redeeming love, and therefore, refused to be aliens and exiles in the radical sense of isolation. From the beginning Christians worked hard at interpreting the words of Jesus: "Give to the emperor the things that are the emperor's, and to God the things that are God's" (Mark 12:17). Each generation of the church must continue to struggle with those words. Second, 1 Peter calls on us to honor, to treat with respect all persons. No one is to be regarded with condescension nor robbed of dignity. Third, love for brothers and sisters in Christ is to remain always intact, and to be nourished. Fourth, reverent fear is reserved for God alone. And finally, the most persuasive witness to one's faith, especially in the face of misunderstanding and criticism, is in the conduct just described. The one area in which this text does not instruct us has to do with the extraordinary way in which we differ from the first readers of this epistle. They were power-less before the government, without vote or voice. We have both voice and vote and can make a difference. What will that difference be? Those Christians in Asia Minor could not begin to imagine the privileges and possibilities that are ours.

A Particular Word to Slaves (1 Peter 2:18–25)

2:18 **Slaves, accept the authority of your masters with all deference, not only those who are kind and gentle but also those who are harsh.** [19] **For it is a credit to you if, being aware of God, you endure pain while suffering unjustly.** [20] **If you endure when you are beaten for doing wrong, what credit is that? But if you endure when you do right and suffer for it, you have God's approval.** [21] **For to this you have been called, because Christ also suffered for you, leaving you an example, so that you should follow in his steps.**
   [22] **"He committed no sin,**
      and no deceit was found in his mouth."
[23] **When he was abused, he did not return abuse; when he suffered, he did not threaten; but he entrusted himself to the one who judges justly.** [24] **He himself bore our sins in his body on the cross, so that, free from sins, we might live for righteousness; by his wounds you have been healed.** [25] **For you were going astray like sheep, but now you have returned to the shep-herd and guardian of your souls.**

This section continues the table of household duties (2:13–3:7). Before proceeding, let us remind ourselves of the structure and nature of a house-hold in that culture. It consisted of the head of the household—usually a man but sometimes a woman (Lydia, Acts 16:14–15)—spouse, children, other relatives temporarily or permanently present, strangers temporarily enjoying the hospitality of the household, servants, tutors and attendants for the children, and slaves. Of course, wealth and the owner's disposition were factors in the size of the household. The Roman government re-garded the household as the foundation of the empire. It was a traditional institution offering stability, food, shelter, education, and a well-defined place for every person there. Whenever the head of a household was, along with the other members of this extended family, converted to Chris-tianity, a house church was formed. And even though hospitality was ex-tended to other Christians for worship and fellowship, the household con-tinued to function as a household (Acts 11:14; 16:14–15; 16:30–34; Rom. 16:3–5; 16:23; 1 Cor. 16:15, 19; Philemon 2). The church, not yet formed into any particular structure, welcomed this institutional form. It gave place, security, and hospitality.

The time came, however, when the church abandoned this structure for a variety of reasons, two of which were prominent. One, the head of the household sometimes exercised too much control; for example, determining rules for extending or not extending hospitality to other Christians (see 2 John 10–11). Two, the place of each person in the household was sometimes too rigidly defined and was seen as contradicting Christian freedom. For example, the wife, the unmarried woman, and the slave often had little room to grow beyond the restricting ways others perceived them. However, at the time 1 Peter was written, this confrontation between the structure and the liberating power of the gospel apparently had not occurred.

Because the full impact of the gospel and its implications for social and political change had not yet been felt, 1 Peter 2:18–25 gives instructions for those in the church who are slaves. The word for slave used here is not the general one but refers to household slaves, domestics. They were not, however, exempt from the verbal and physical abuse inflicted on all slaves. Ordinarily a table of household duties included both slaves and masters, but here no word is given to masters. Why? Were there no slave owners in the churches of Asia Minor? Or does the writer simply have nothing to say to those who own others? One immediately recalls the teaching of Jesus. His instruction was to those who were forced to go a mile, but he had no word for those who did the forcing. He advised those taken to court but not those who brought them there. He spoke to those struck on the cheek, but we know of no saying from him to those who strike others. Apparently Jesus' followers were the abused, not the abusers. Perhaps that is true in the case of slaves and not slave owners in the churches addressed by 1 Peter. But whatever the reason, it is important that we have no word here to masters, because in the history of slavery, it has been slave owners and sellers who used this text as biblical support for slavery. It was not written to them or for them. It was written to those who were slaves, had become Christians, but were still slaves.

Because the gospel and the better angels of human nature have moved us past slavery to the point of amazement that such an institution ever existed, there is no way that anything the author says will be satisfactory to us. But if we listen in, perhaps something said will carry in it a principle portable to our circumstance and worthy of emulation. The recipients have already been told that they are God's slaves; they are in the service of God (2:16). This does not, of course, release them from human bondage but it does relativize human servitude. Dignity and worth in God's love alters how one faces and lives through a difficult day. That both writer and reader believed that "the end of all things is near" (4:7) also affected the way every human condition, including slavery, was experienced. Both joy and sorrow were fleeting, and so little thought was given to long-range plans to improve society. These slaves have also been told they are free (2:16). Someone in bondage could hear that message as mere words having little to do with "the way things really are," but the history of slavery is the history of men and women claiming and expressing in countless ways freedom of the human spirit. To know that one is a child of God gives one a voice to say, "I belong to God; what can anyone do to me?" When chains fall off the spirit, that fact alone threatens the whole institution of slavery.

Of unusual significance is the writer's reminder to the slaves that their behavior is not to be determined by the master, reacting one way to the gentle, another to the cruel (v. 18). The life of the Christian is determined by God and is not a reaction to the conduct or attitude of another. Jesus said this very thing to all of us, slave or free. You are not, he said, to love the neighbor and hate the enemy, speak to the friendly but not the unfriendly, be generous to the generous but withhold from the selfish. No, God acts out of God's own nature, never reacting, but sending sun and rain on both the just and the unjust. Likewise you are not to react, allowing others to determine your actions and attitudes; rather, you are to be children of your father in heaven (Matt. 5:43–48). Of course, such an orientation will cause one to suffer even when doing what is right, but such was the life of Jesus (v. 21). At this point in the discussion, the author holds before the slaves a portrait of Jesus of Nazareth, saying: Live this way, walk in his steps.

The portrait of Jesus drawn here relies heavily on the description of God's suffering servant in Isaiah 53. In fact, the formal qualities of 2:21b–25 suggest an early Christian hymn based on Isa. 53:4–12. Verse 22 actually quotes Isa. 53:9 (in a Greek translation of the Hebrew) and the remainder of the passage is filled with allusions to the suffering servant. Three clear christological ideas vital to the church are expressed here. First, there is Christ the example. He suffered unjustly but without retaliation. He was treated as a slave, and his response to that treatment provides an example for the readers. What did Jesus do under circumstances similar to ours is a question asked by Christians then and now, and the Gospel accounts of Jesus' life have been read by many with this question in mind. What Jesus did and what Jesus said, to the extent that these are available to us, have always been two primary resources for ethical decision making in the church. Second, this text presents Christ the redeemer. Reminiscent of Col. 1:22, verse 24 gives a classic statement of the redeeming death of Christ. The death of Christ is not presented as a call to martyrdom but as a reminder to Christian slaves that they have been set free from sin in order to live righteously. And finally, this passage speaks of Christ the sustainer. You are not alone, says the writer. Christ continues with you as shepherd (cf. 5:4) and as guardian, that is, as your guide, caretaker, and overseer ("guardian" translates *episkopos*, the usual word for "bishop").

To those of us who find the instructions to slaves too cautious, lacking the boldness of Christian freedom, two words are in order. First, without justifying any form of oppression and not at all championing acquiescence, it is appropriate to remember that restraint can be as much an exercise of freedom as revolution. Parents for the sake of children, friends for the sake of friends, and mature Christians for the sake of the newly baptized often refrain from a full demand for and exercise of rights. Paul sometimes argued for his rights and then explained why he did not make full use of these rights. As he put it, "For though I am free with respect to all, I have made myself a slave to all, so that I might win more of them" (1 Cor. 9:19).

Second, let us not feel superior as though we came out of our baptism full grown and completely aware of all the freedoms we have been granted. These understandings often come embarrassingly slowly. Accepting non-Jews in the church was a real problem for Simon Peter and many other members of the first church. It is difficult to believe that women did not gain the right to vote until the twentieth century. Some bodies of Christians are still debating whether to open their pulpits to women. I had occasion recently to read a book I wrote only twenty years ago, and in it I said repeatedly, "The minister, *he*. . . ." Truth dawns so slowly, and we grow so unevenly, quite open on one matter and quite closed on a companion idea. We are set free of one prejudice and immediately develop a prejudice against those still prejudiced. Let us be gracious to one another, surprised and grateful for signs of maturing, humbled by the distance yet to go.

A Particular Word to Wives (1 Peter 3:1–6)

3:1 **Wives, in the same way, accept the authority of your husbands, so that, even if some of them do not obey the word, they may be won over without a word by their wives' conduct, 2 when they see the purity and reverence** of your lives. [3] **Do not adorn yourselves outwardly by braiding your hair and by wearing gold ornaments or fine clothing;** [4] **rather, let your adornment be the inner self with the lasting beauty of a gentle and quiet spirit, which is very precious in God's sight.** [5] **It was in this way long ago that the holy women who hoped in God used to adorn themselves by accepting the authority of their husbands.** [6] **Thus Sarah obeyed Abraham and called him lord. You have become her daughters as long as you do what is good and never let fears alarm you.**

The table of household duties continues with 3:1 parallel to 2:18; that is, as slaves were to accept the authority of their masters so wives were to accept the authority of their husbands. Literally, the text says "your own husbands" (see Eph. 5:22) as though to avoid calling for subordination to all men. Likewise, as the behavior of slaves was not to be determined by the character and disposition of masters, so the conduct of wives was not to be in response to their husbands' being Christian or not. Some members of the church at Corinth had written to Paul inquiring about a similar matter. Should a Christian married to an unbeliever continue in that marriage? Paul's advice was to stay married if the unbelieving spouse consented; the happy consequence might be the conversion of the spouse and the Christian education of the children (1 Cor. 7:12–16). So the writer of 1 Peter is confident of the persuasive power of a Christian life (2:12) even "without a word" (v. 1); that is, without preaching to the husband. Even though the text says "some" of the husbands were not believers, one gets the impression that most of the wives had been converted without their husbands, else why dwell as such length on the matter? We can only imagine the tensions created in the homes where wives had not observed the long tradition of the empire, that a wife follows her husband in religion. We may have a hint of domestic strife in verse 6: "never let fears alarm you." This expression draws on Prov. 3:25, which speaks of not allowing oneself to be terrorized. Might this not indicate intimidation and threats from unbelieving husbands? If so, the response advised is to live in purity and reverence, keep a gentle and quiet spirit, and accept the husband's authority. Implied in the instruction, however, is that one is not to relinquish one's faith because a domineering and threatening husband demands it. If the line is drawn there, we have no word from the writer to wives who might find themselves divorced by such husbands. Paul's advice was: Stay with your spouse but if he (or she) divorces you, then you are no longer under obligation; you are free (1 Cor. 7:15).

The advice against fine clothing, gold jewelry, and braided hair leaves us with a question. Were these wives engaged in making visible their new freedom in Christ, moving out of the submissive and simple life in the household and attending to appearances in public? Or is it rather the case that the wives addressed happened to be married to men of means? Slaves and domestic workers do not need to be told that fine gowns, expensive jewelry, and visits to beauticians are inappropriate. Whatever the case, 1 Peter joins many philosophers and moral teachers of the day who found luxury and ostentation incompatible with the pursuit of the higher life of the spirit. The writer finds precedent for the simple life of inner beauty in the holy women of the past. These women, Sarah being but one example, set their hope in God, and with that governing principle, chose the beauty which was "lasting." This word translates a favorite of the writer's: imperishable, incorruptible (1:4, 7, 18, 23). While these instructions to Christian wives may seem at first out of date and quaint, at the heart of it is a principle that followers of Christ, both women and men, have taken to be timeless. To be overly concerned with how one appears to others, or to find one's identity and self-confidence in adornment, especially when the expenditure involved is in sharp contrast to the scenes of poverty and hunger all around us, is incompatible with the life and teaching of Jesus of Nazareth. This is not a call to wear the hair shirt, but waste, no matter how dazzling, is still waste.

A Particular Word to Husbands (1 Peter 3:7)

3:7 **Husbands, in the same way, show consideration for your wives in your life together, paying honor to the woman as the weaker sex, since they too are also heirs of the gracious gift of life—so that nothing may hinder your prayers.**

With brief remarks to husbands the table of household duties concludes. These are not the unbelieving husbands of the Christian wives addressed above, but they are themselves Christians and obviously married to believing women. The brevity of the instructions does not imply, as some have suggested, that men had less difficulty adjusting to church life than did women. What is not simply implied but rather obvious is the increased benefit and blessing when both husband and wife are Christian. But even with a believing spouse, a husband had to make major adjustments in his relation to her. Accustomed to great authority over a wife and the entire household, he now had to reinterpret all his relationships, and he had to do so without a model or precedent or even encouragement in society. No doubt he had support within the church, but even there he lacked the guidance of prior generations of Christian men. There was not yet a New Testament, and so letters like this from Christian leaders must have been welcomed and helpful. It is difficult if not impossible for us who create a Christian home well resourced by church history, family background, scriptures, church fellowship, informed leadership, and a favorable society to imagine the halting and awkward beginning steps of first-generation Christians in Asia Minor. The advice to husbands may seem elementary, and so it is, but it is also basic and not yet outdated. Listen to what is said and discern whether the words might still be appropriate.

Husbands, "show consideration for your wives." Literally, the expression calls for regarding wives "according to knowledge"; that is, knowledge of God. In other words, let your understanding of God be the guide in relating to your wives. Remember that your lives are together. You are partners in the home. You are not to take advantage of her or try to lord it over her simply because she is not physically as strong as you are. Rather you are to respect her, seeing her value as a person and not as an extension of yourself. This is the meaning of the word "honor" as in wedding vows that say, "Will you love and honor . . .?" After all, husbands and wives are joint heirs of God's grace. Before the gracious act of God in Christ no one is second class. If, then, you share life in this way, there will be no obstacle to your growth in matters of the spirit. Even your prayers will be joined and rise as one to God.

Frankly, after listening to this, time and place fall away and the words sound appropriate both for those approaching marriage and for those who may need a refresher course on how to be a husband.

And a Word to All (1 Peter 3:8–12)

3:8 Finally, all of you, have unity of spirit, sympathy, love for one another, a tender heart, and a humble mind. 9 Do not repay evil for evil or abuse for abuse; but, on the contrary, repay with a blessing. It is for this that you were called—that you might inherit a blessing, 10 For
　　"Those who desire life
　　　　and desire to see good days,
　　let them keep their tongues from evil
　　　　and their lips from speaking deceit;
　　11 let them turn away from evil and do good;
　　　　let them seek peace and pursue it.
　　12 For the eyes of the Lord are on the righteous,
　　　　and his ears are open to their prayer.
　　But the face of the Lord is against those who do evil."

The significance of this unit does not consist of its adding anything new to the discussion thus far. On the contrary, verses 8–12 are a summary of what has been said regarding Christian behavior. Verse 8 describes life as it should be within the fellowship: mutual love, singlemindedness, sympathy, tenderness, and humility. Verse 9 recalls what had earlier been said to slaves concerning behavior toward hostile outsiders (2:18–25): never retaliate but respond with a blessing. All that is said here echoes the teaching of Jesus in the Sermon on the Mount (Matt. 5:38–48), but the phrasing of it recalls Paul (for example, Rom. 12:17; 1 Cor. 4:12; Rom. 12:14). And, as he has done before, the writer strengthens his position with a quotation from the Old Testament. Again he returns to a favorite, Psalm 34, citing at length (vv. 12–16) a psalm used earlier (2:3). However, in 1 Peter the psalm means much more than the psalmist had in mind, for in the hands of Christians, references to "life" and "good days" point to "all this and heaven, too."

What, then, is the significance of this passage? It lies within the Christian modification of the table of household duties. In that culture, each person in the household was addressed, outlining duties peculiar to that person's station or role in the household. However, with the community of faith that is not the end of the matter. When the writer says, "Finally, all of you," he is placing each person back into the fellowship. Individual advice is not enough; they are a church, and only as a church can individuals grow and fulfill the life given to them. It is not enough simply to say that only by staying together could they survive. This letter is to churches, to congregations, and not to individuals because it is the church, the community, which is the body of Christ in the world, the temple made of living stones, the household of faith. The whole is more than the sum of its parts. Only by departure from biblical understanding of the people of God can anyone say, "I am a Christian, but it is a private matter. The church for me is optional." And so, as if to correct any possible misunderstanding that might come from addressing individuals in the household, the author says, Yes it is difficult being a slave or a wife or a husband, all of you being new to the faith and living in an abusive society. But remember, we are church, we support and care for each other, and it is as church that we witness to and reach out to the world. It is a common but sad observation that many among us have not yet understood and enjoyed this sustaining community of faith. Why do the Smiths not attend church anymore? Well, they are having trouble in their marriage. Why has Harry dropped out of our Sunday school class? You see, Harry lost his job and has been unemployed for eight months. I never see Charles and Mary in worship anymore. Why? I guess you have not heard that their daughter is undergoing treatment for drug addiction. Time and again, in case after case, when the church needs to be church for some of its members, the members pull away as though church exists only for those who do not need it. Who or what has created this impression that the fellowship of the church does not include those with problems? Whoever or whatever, the impression is deeply fixed. Often the first act of troubled members is to drop out. Of course, now and then someone clearly has gotten the point. Frances was a faithful and lively member of our Bible study class. Within ten days after an auto accident in which Frances was hurt and her mother killed, she was back in the class. When some in the group expressed surprise that she was there, Frances replied, "Where else should I be? Isn't this my church? I have no other place like this."

Perhaps we still can help each other hear the ancient admonition: "Finally, all of you, have unity of spirit, sympathy, love for one another, a tender heart, and a humble mind."

CHRISTIANS AS SUFFERERS IN THE WORLD
1 Peter 3:13–5:11

The image of Christ's followers suffering dominates this entire section. It is not as though the subject has just now come up; in fact, here the writer elaborates on themes introduced earlier (1:6; 2:12, 15–20; 3:9), but now the fact of suffering gives 3:13–5:11 its character. Some students of 1 Peter, observing the frequent appearance of forms of the word *pascho* ("suffer"), have been persuaded that 1 Peter is a paschal liturgy or homily and so have imagined its use at Good Friday or Easter when the church remembers the suffering of Christ. This is an interesting but not overwhelming theory. What is undeniably true, however, is that the suffering of Christ is the centerpiece in the discussion of suffering among Christians. Anxious believers, looking out on a hostile society, brutal in its abuse, hunger for a word of explanation, of encouragement, of meaning. The writer's best response is to point them to the cross and empty tomb.

We need to bear in mind that the suffering which occupies our attention here is not suffering in general: the pains of age and disease, birth defects, the effects of drought, floods, storms, plagues, and the other misery-inflicting forces sometimes referred to as "natural evil." These causes of suffering are never far from us and sooner or later raise for many of us questions about the will and goodness of God. From the days of Job until today the discussion goes on. Jesus' disciples asked him to interpret the case of a man born blind (John 9:1–2), and persons in his audience wanted his help in understanding random killings and accidental deaths (Luke 13:1–5). Of course they wanted to know; we want to know. However, in the text before us is the issue of suffering at the hands of others, suffering intentionally inflicted on Christians by their neighbors. Why the verbal abuse, the social ostracism, the painful rumors, the charges of wrongdoing, the anonymous pamphlets, the many faces of hatred? The text presents such mistreatment as very intense and very present (4:12). The Christians listen for an interpretation of what is happening, for instructions on how to respond, and for a word of hope.

While Doing What Is Right (1 Peter 3:13–17)

3:13 **Now who will harm you if you are eager to do what is good?** [14] **But even if you do suffer for doing what is right, you are blessed. Do not fear what they fear, and do not be intimidated,** [15] **but in your hearts sanctify Christ as Lord. Always be ready to make your defense to anyone who demands from you an accounting for the hope that is in you;** [16] **yet do it with gentleness and reverence. Keep your conscience clear, so that, when you are maligned, those who abuse you for your good conduct in Christ may be put to shame.** [17] **For it is better to suffer for doing good, if suffering should be God's will, than to suffer for doing evil.**

In this unit the writer enlarges for all the members what had already been said to slaves and wives who suffer abuse because of their stations in the household and in society. Verse 13 picks up on the closing phrase of verse 12, "those who do evil" (quoted from Psalm 34:16) but moves with it in a different direction. The message offered to the sufferers, practical and straightforward, never seems to depart from two assumptions that history has demonstrated to be rather idealistic: One, if you are truly engaged in doing what is right, you will not be harmed; in fact, you will be protected by the government (2:14). Experience has shown, however—and the writer does acknowledge it (vv. 14, 16, and again at 4:14–16)—that some are abused, not in spite of their doing right but precisely because they are. What the accusations against Christians in Asia Minor were are not known for sure. We do know that because the Christians did not believe in and worship the array of Roman gods they were called "atheists." That term carried with it a cluster of prejudices against Christians that questioned their character, citizenship, patriotism, and social responsibility. It remains the case that to call a person an "atheist" is, in the popular mind, to imply many negative qualities about that person which may not be true at all. Those Christians who did not, for conscience' sake, eat meat that had been dedicated to idols could be charged with an economic boycott. And, as was said earlier, Christians loving each other could easily be misconstrued, as could also the sacrament of the body and blood of Jesus. But whatever the specific charges, the fact was and is that acts of caring and generosity as well as consistent devotion to telling the truth arouse opposition. Love seems to stir hatred in those who refuse to love. Falsehood works hardest to be persuasive if the truth is released in a room. And peace is always a threat to the purse of those who profit from war. "Why would anyone kill the priest?" they asked. "He was a good, gentle man who loved our children and was helping to rid our neighborhood of drugs." They have answered their own question.

The second assumption of the writer is that conduct which is Christian is persuasive, sometimes converting the abuser (2:12), sometimes silencing the critic (2:15), and sometimes putting to shame the opponent whose accusation is shown to be patently false (3:16). The word "sometimes" should be underscored. While a deed often speaks louder than words and we know of case after case of the positive power of Christian character, many critics and cynics, in the face of such behavior, merely change the attack. It may now be an accusation of being pious, or holy, or righteous, or religious, words that have joined a number of others stolen from the church's vocabulary and soiled on the street. We might as well face it: We are called to be responsible for our actions but not for the reactions of others.

For the church under such heavy social duress, the writer has clear and strong advice. Do not, says verse 13, be passive in goodness and think you have achieved Christian character by reason of the list of things you do not do. Be eager for the good; that is, take initiative, overcome evil with good. The expression "eager to do" translates "be zealots" for good. There is no reason to let the word "zealot" lead us to assume that members of the church were engaged in zealotic, that is, politically rebellious activity and the writer wants that energy redirected. What is being advised is that neither their minority status nor the social hostility be allowed to produce in them moral timidity. Rather claim the blessing pronounced by Christ himself: "Blessed are those who are persecuted for righteousness' sake, for theirs is the kingdom of heaven" (Matt. 5:10). In verses 14b–15a the readers are called to courage. Drawing on Isa. 8:12–13, the writer says not to quake before secular power nor be intimidated by those who claim to hold your life in their hands. Only the Lord is to be feared; only the

Lord is to be hallowed. But be ready for the unexpected. Someone may interrogate you about the hope within you. (Hope here refers to one's entire faith stance rather than simply to the hope of an afterlife.) You should be able to offer a defense of the gospel you have embraced. We have no clue as to whether the questioning was by private citizens or public officials. In any case, think through your answer ahead of time lest you and the church be embarrassed either by your frightened silence or your empty enthusiasm. (To help believers articulate their new faith, creedal formulations arose early in the life of the church, as the New Testament testifies—1 Cor. 8:6; 2 Cor. 8:9; Phil. 2:6–11; Col. 1:15–20; Heb. 1:1–4; and others.) However, when you do witness, do so with gentleness and respect. Nothing is so alienating and obnoxious as Christian witnessing with arrogance and condescension, with rudeness and intrusion. Have a sense of the appropriate. The governor Pliny later complained that Christians he investigated were stubborn and obstinate. Have courage, yes, but do not hinder the gentle progress of the gospel with your attitude, and do not irritate your listeners as though you were trying to draw their fire. There is no need to make your own cross; if God wills, you will suffer soon enough. Here "God's will" is not to be heard as a harsh sound, burdensome to endure. It was among early Christians considered a special privilege to be in that inner circle who were called on to experience what Christ experienced. As the writer will say at 4:13, "But rejoice insofar as you are sharing Christ's sufferings." Or as Paul expressed it to the Philippians: "And this is God's doing. For he has graciously granted you the privilege not only of believing in Christ, but of suffering for him as well" (1:28–29). There have always been in the church those who ran from any suffering asked of them, and there have always been those who ran toward suffering, seeking wounds in order to identify with Jesus. The former are cowardly; the latter are sick. The writer of 1 Peter understands Christian suffering as being God's invitation. Those who joined the fellowship of suffering were later to be referred to as "the friends of God."

Defined by the Passion and Resurrection of Jesus (1 Peter 3:18–4:2)

3:18 For Christ also suffered for sins once for all, the righteous for the unrighteous, in order to bring you to God. He was put to death in the flesh, but made alive in the spirit, 19 in which also he went and made a proclamation to the spirits in prison, 20 who in former times did not obey, when God waited patiently in the days of Noah, during the building of the ark, in

which a few, that is, eight persons, were saved through water. [21] **And baptism, which this prefigured, now saves you—not as a removal of dirt from the body, but as an appeal to God for a good conscience, through the resurrection of Jesus Christ,** [22] **who has gone into heaven and is at the right hand of God, with angels, authorities, and powers made subject to him.**

4:1 Since therefore Christ suffered in the flesh, arm yourselves also with the same intention (for whoever has suffered in the flesh has finished with sin), [2] **so as to live for the rest of your earthly life no longer by human desires but by the will of God.**

Again, the subject of the suffering of believers at the hands of unbelievers turns the attention of writer and readers to the suffering of Christ. In addressing the mistreatment endured by Christian slaves, the author concluded the discussion by reminding them of the undeserved mistreatment of Christ (2:19–25). In the twenty centuries of Christian history, thousands of sermons, lectures, and books have probed the problem of the unjust suffering of God's people, but no response to the issue—philosophical, theological, or practical—has ministered to the victims quite like the reminder of the crucified Christ. In this one image there can be found the God who suffers with us, love that endures rather than avoids pain, companionship with Jesus Christ, fellowship with others who gather at the cross, a sense that in the larger scheme of things even suffering can have meaning, and the sure hope of life beyond suffering through the resurrection of the crucified Christ. It is fitting and proper that we return again and again to the passion and resurrection of Christ, in both pain and joy.

The reader will also recall that at 2:19–25 when the writer spoke of the suffering of Christ, he did so by using a hymn or creedal formula (2:21–25). We observed at that point that it was not uncommon in the New Testament to find christological hymns imbedded in practical and pastoral discussions of Christian conduct. By way of reminder, look at the hymn to Christ in Phil. 2:6–11, a hymn prompted by Paul's advice concerning church members being servants of one another. So here, the pastoral concern for believers who are maligned unjustly leads the writer to quote a christological hymn (3:18–22) that may or may not have been familiar to the readers. That these verses do constitute a hymn has been widely recognized by students of 1 Peter. Although English translations do not make visible the poetic form, the most recent Greek New Testament prints these verses as one would present a poem and the formal, liturgical nature of the passage is quite evident.

Other than reminding us that early Christians rather quickly cast their faith in hymns and creeds, what does the fact that verses 18–22 are a christological poem contribute to our understanding of the passage? Several observations are in order. First, because these hymns are confessions of faith, they are digests of the substance of what Christians believed, and therefore every phrase is rich and full of meaning. A quick glance at another christological hymn (1 Tim. 3:16) will make apparent how the whole gospel can be contained in so small a space.

> He was revealed in flesh,
>   vindicated in spirit,
>   seen by angels,
>   proclaimed among Gentiles,
>   believed in throughout the world,
>   taken up in glory.

Second, even though an entire hymn, or at least a stanza, is quoted, the contribution of the piece to the matter being discussed may involve only one item in the hymn. This is to say, not all parts of the quotation are equally important to the writer's immediate purpose and, therefore, may not call for equal treatment in a commentary. Finally, and perhaps most importantly, because the hymn contains in brief the whole of the church's affirmation about Christ, that fact guards against the reduction of Christology to the need of the moment. For example, to a church involved in issues of social justice, Christ may be viewed as a political activist; to another heavily invested in spirituality, Christ may be appropriated as a person of prayer; to others convinced of the centrality of education, Christ is the teacher; while yet others may see him through their need for a friend of the poor, or a liberator of women, or a mystic visionary, or a triumphant Lord. All these images and others contain truth about Christ, but to claim for any one of them the whole truth would be reductionistic. In the case of 1 Peter, the pressure to say a word of encouragement to sufferers could seduce a writer into a suffering-Jesus Christology, but as we shall see, that pitfall is avoided by quoting a hymn that presents a suffering Christ to be sure but also a Christ who is larger than the immediate need of the reader. The important function of the hymn is to prevent Christology from being totally consumed by the need of one particular community of believers. As dull and irrelevant as doctrine may seem to some, these professions of faith guard the church against defining the Christian religion totally in terms of a problem we happen to face today.

And so, says our text, in your suffering look to Jesus the innocent martyr. This portrait of Jesus as an innocent ("righteous" in v. 18 is elsewhere translated "innocent," Matt. 27:19; Luke 23:47) sufferer allows suffering believers to identify with him. Quite early in Christian preaching the image of Jesus as a martyr, the righteous (or "just," v. 18 in REB) at the hands of the unrighteous, was already firmly imbedded (Acts 3:14; 7:52; 22:14). But his suffering has meaning beyond that of his followers because his affliction was not only *by* sinners but also *for* sinners. It has been this conviction which has enabled the church to view the passion of Christ as tragic, yes, but as lying beyond tragedy. What does the writer say of his death? It was vicarious (the righteous for the unrighteous); it was atoning (suffered for sins; also Heb. 9:28); it was reconciling (in order to bring you to God; also Eph. 3:12; Heb. 7:25); and it was sufficient for our salvation, never needing to be repeated (once for all; also Rom. 6:10; Heb. 9:26). The New Testament and subsequent Christian history is filled with images, analogies, and figures of speech attempting to clarify for readers of many backgrounds and cultures the saving effect of Christ's death, and yet it remains what 1 Tim. 3:16 calls "the mystery of our religion." That Christ died is a fact of history; that Christ died for our sins is an affirmation of faith. Paul never ceased to be amazed by this centerpiece of all his preaching. Near the end of his ministry he wrote: "For while we were still weak, at the right time Christ died for the ungodly. Indeed, rarely will anyone die for a righteous person—though perhaps for a good person someone might actually dare to die. But God proves his love for us in that while we still were sinners Christ died for us" (Rom. 5:6–8).

The hymn in verses 18–22 thus takes the readers out of a preoccupation with their own suffering as they sing the praises of one who "was put to death in the flesh, but made alive in the spirit" (v. 18). As the governor Pliny said in his letter to the Emperor Trajan, these Christians meet early in the morning and sing hymns to Christ. But now the hymn in 1 Peter moves the reader beyond self, beyond the community, beyond Asia Minor, to contemplate the cosmic significance of the death and resurrection of Christ. The Christian faith is personal, to be sure, but it is not private, and whoever tries to confine the full meaning of the gospel "in my heart" has cast the story on too small a screen. Our text joins many others in the New Testament in affirming that the redeeming work of Christ is cosmic in its scope, as broad as all creation, uniting heaven and earth, and offering reconciliation to all creatures visible and invisible (Eph. 1:20–22; Phil. 2:9–11; Col. 1:15–20). The expression "he went and made a proclamation to the spirits in prison" (v. 19; also 4:6: "the gospel was proclaimed even to the dead") prompts us to pause and try to think as did the composer of this hymn to Christ.

Christians have from the beginning believed that there is no scarcity to the love of God. It is God's desire that the realm of redemption be as broad as the realm of creation. Creation, many believed, included not only human beings and the earth they occupy but also invisible beings created by God for maintaining life and order in the world (Heb. 1:7–14). These creatures are variously called angels, powers, spirits, principalities, and authorities (v. 22; also 1 Cor. 15:24–28; Eph. 3:7–10; Col. 1:15–16). These beings, like human beings, rebelled against God and, therefore, were in need of reconciliation if God's creation was to be restored to its original harmony. While human beings dwell on earth, these creatures, said our forebears, dwell not only on earth but under the earth and in the heavens (v. 22; also Phil. 2:10). Much of this sounds strange to many of us, for our world is very much an "it" and impersonal, not a "they," alive and mysteriously populated. However, I do recall as a boy being instructed by an elderly woman of our rural community that the water well in our back yard had to be kept covered. When I asked why, expecting a warning about the danger of falling in, she told me that after dark, spirits would come up through the well from the world below. These spirits, she said, might burn down a barn, or wither a garden, or perhaps harm a baby. One night, awakened by the memory of having left the well uncovered, I rushed out to replace the lid. After waiting in silent fear for several days, expecting a calamity for which I would have been responsible, I finally comforted myself with the belief that I had covered the well before the spirits could exit.

When one places within this worldview the conviction that the saving work of Christ was for all creation, then it follows that the lordship of Christ, to be fully effective, must be extended not only on earth but also under the earth and in the heavens. This is the assertion of verse 22. Perhaps Paul has put it more vividly when he quotes, in Phil. 2:9–11, a hymn to Christ very similar to our text:

> Therefore God also highly exalted him
>   and gave him the name
>   that is above every name,
> so that at the name of Jesus
>   every knee should bend,
>   in heaven and on earth and under the earth,
> and every tongue should confess
>   that Jesus Christ is Lord,
>   to the glory of God the Father.

Let us return to the conviction that Christ is God's saving act "once for all." This means that the benefits of his death are not only extended spatially (in the heavens, on earth, and under the earth) but also temporally; that is, for all time. But what of those who died prior to the event of Jesus Christ? It follows that to them a proclamation of the good news had to be made. That, says the writer, was accomplished by Christ after he had been put to death in the flesh but was still alive in the spirit. As the Apostles' Creed states it, "he descended into hell." The text does not broadly refer to everyone who lived "in former times" (v. 20) but focuses on those in Noah's time. The reasons for this may be several. First, the unbelieving and disobedient in the days of Noah represent another world, a world destroyed due to evil and hence may symbolize all in the past who need a word from God. Second, since the people of Noah's time are characterized as the most grossly evil (Genesis 6), it can be assumed that if grace is offered to them, it is surely offered to everyone. And finally, since the Christ hymn is being used for the newly baptized (the hymn might have been composed for a baptismal service), the Noah story (Genesis 6—8) provides an analogy for baptism.

The analogy between Noah's ark and baptism must not be pressed too far. After all, Noah and family were saved by not being in the water, quite unlike the baptized. But water is involved in both and both are saved by the act of God. Baptism's effect is certainly not physical; it is not a bath. The NRSV translates verse 21b, "an appeal to God for a good conscience." It is a difficult expression. The REB says "the appeal made to God from a good conscience." Literally the passage can be translated "an appeal (or request) of a good conscience to God." Heb. 10:22 speaks similarly of baptism: "Let us approach with a true heart in full assurance of faith, with our hearts sprinkled clean from an evil conscience and our bodies washed with pure water." At any rate, the writer is as confident as Paul (Rom. 6:1–11) that in baptism, a re-enactment of the death and resurrection of Christ, the believer appropriates the benefits of Christ's sacrifice in our behalf.

When the church seeks to express in today's terms and categories the convictions of this hymn, it suffers from the poverty of language. Christ is Lord of all life. The truth about God revealed in the death and resurrection of Jesus Christ is that no one—past, present, or future—lies outside or beyond that seeking and saving love. In fact, not only human life but all life is the object of God's care. Thoughtless exploitation of earth, sea, and sky are therefore acts contrary to the love and providence of God. And while a modern worldview may not include hostile angels, principalities, and powers, one would be naive and blind to miss the presence among us of forces organized and unorganized that oppress, dehumanize, exploit, and violate in ways covert and overt, driven by greed and power sometimes flaunted, sometimes concealed in pleasing words and gestures of benevolence. Until these forces are made subject to the exalted and reigning Christ (v. 22), none of us are totally free of their influence, even when we think our actions are prompted by unselfish motives. We have not yet grown past the need to hear again the opening line of the hymn to Christ: "For Christ also suffered for sins . . . in order to bring you [us] to God."

Following the hymn, the writer draws a moral lesson from it in the manner of a preacher who explains a biblical text and then exhorts the listeners with thoughts found in the passage. In this case the hymn to Christ (vv. 18–22) is the writer's "text." However, not all of it is directly applied to the readers. The entirety of 3:18–22 serves to create the faith world of the believers; it expresses the whole of the Christ event and thus reminds the church what it means to live, as Paul would say, "in Christ." But for the moral application the writer returns only to verse 18, which, by speaking of Christ's suffering, touched the readers most directly at the point of their present experience of abuse. The lesson (4:1–2) is clear and straightforward: Just as Christ by his suffering was severed from sin and joined to God, so you also should let your suffering make you dead to sin and alive to God. In other words, let your suffering serve as a rite of passage. Like your baptism, the time of pain can mark a transition from the old life to the new life. Pain and hardship do not automatically have positive effects. That is, suffering does not in and of itself make one more moral, more faithful, more Christian. And it is not likely that the writer wishes to imply that in the parenthetical comment, "for whoever has suffered in the flesh has finished with sin" (v. 1). It could be that he means nothing deeply theological but is speaking more practically. For example, suffering tends to burn out of us those desires that hinder the life of the spirit, or suffering sobers us and becomes the occasion for recovering values lost or neglected. But we know from our own experience and by observation of others that suffering does not always have such positive effect. Some are embittered, distanced from God, and filled with new doubts about divine providence.

When viewed theologically, suffering has been regarded by some Christians and Jews as paying the price for sin, as in the proverb, "Death cancels all debts." When martyrdom was a fact in the church, sought by some, avoided by others, some theologians held that martyrdom itself atoned for sin and awarded forgiveness. But in our text there is no claim for intrinsic value in suffering as a Christian. When the writer says "whoever has suffered in the flesh has finished with sin" he is not saying that suffering gives one merit before God, atones for sin, and provides access to heaven. Rather, it is more likely that the text is an echo of a passage in Paul's letter already familiar to the church in Rome, from which 1 Peter was written. One difference is noticeable: In the Roman letter conversion is described as *death* and new life. Listen to Rom. 6:7–11 as the possible background for 1 Peter 4:1–2: "For whoever has died is freed from sin. But if we have died with Christ, we believe that we will also live with him. . . . The death he [Christ] died, he died to sin, once for all; but the life he lives, he lives to God. So you also must consider yourselves dead to sin and alive to God in Christ Jesus." Even if there is no literary relationship between Romans and 1 Peter, still there could hardly be found anywhere a better commentary on 1 Peter 4:1–2.

Living in the Will of God (1 Peter 4:3–11)

4:3 **You have already spent enough time in doing what the Gentiles like to do, living in licentiousness, passions, drunkenness, revels, carousing, and lawless idolatry. 4 They are surprised that you no longer join them in the same excesses of dissipation, and so they blaspheme. 5 But they will have to give an accounting to him who stands ready to judge the living and the dead. 6 For this is the reason the gospel was proclaimed even to the dead, so that, though they had been judged in the flesh as everyone is judged, they might live in the spirit as God does.**

7 The end of all things is near; therefore be serious and discipline yourselves for the sake of your prayers. 8 Above all, maintain constant love for one another, for love covers a multitude of sins. 9 Be hospitable to one another without complaining. 10 Like good stewards of the manifold grace of God, serve one another with whatever gift each of you has received. 11 Whoever speaks must do so as one speaking the very words of God; whoever serves must do so with the strength that God supplies, so that God may be glorified in all things through Jesus Christ. To him belong the glory and the power forever and ever. Amen.

Having introduced the will of God as the governing consideration for the Christian life, the writer now elaborates on what that means for the believing community. The elaboration was and is needed. One wearies of being exhorted and urged to do God's will, but with no clue as to what that might be. It is not often that the clouds part and the will of God in a given situation comes through as clear as the morning sun. In general terms, yes, we can discern God's will by reflecting on the nature of God as revealed in Jesus Christ. We can be rather certain that some behavior and relationships are in harmony with the love and care of God and that some are not. But in many concrete circumstances decisions have to be made, courses of action taken, in which what is and what seems can hardly be distinguished. At such times our world turns into Gethsemane, we struggle, we ask friends to watch with us and pray, and we search the scriptures. Surely the first readers of 1 Peter were grateful for the writer's extended comments on the will of God.

What, then, is it to live by the will of God? First, it means to be done with the former life. Having set up the language of contrast in verse 2 (human desires vs. will of God), the writer continues in this vein through verse 6 (in the flesh vs. in the spirit). A good deal of attention is given to the former life, "doing what the Gentiles like to do," painting it in vivid and ugly colors. No doubt that way of life, encountered by the church members every day, still had for some a strong drawing power, especially when neighbors and friends "are surprised that you no longer join them" (v. 4). At the beginning of the second century when a government investigation in Asia Minor found quite a number who confessed to having once been Christians but were no longer, no doubt some of the casualties fell to the former way of life. The catalog of sins attributed to the Gentiles need not be taken as a biographical sketch of the prebaptism life of the addressees. This is a general characterization of what Greeks called "barbarian life." Among Jews, Greek moralists, and Christians there were "vice lists" used to portray behavior regarded as totally unacceptable. Such lists occur frequently in the New Testament (Rom. 1:29–31; 1 Cor. 6:9–10; Gal. 5:19–21; Rev. 21:8). And if any of the believers were being seduced into thinking that such behavior was escaping God's attention, the reminder of God's judgment closes this phase of the discussion. God's judgment will be universal. It will be based on one's conduct, but it will not be vengeful or vindictive. Rather, God's grace remains available to all, the living and the dead (cf. the discussion at 3:19–20). Christians who tend to be judgmental of others rather than leaving them to God should note here the absence of any triumphant screams over the fence at outsiders.

Second, living by the will of God involves a number of specific attitudes and patterns of behavior. The writer enters this discussion through an archway that is inscribed, "The end of all things is near" (v. 7). This conviction, widely shared in the early church (Mark 9:1; 1 Cor. 7:29–31; Phil. 4—5; 1 Thess. 5:6; James 5:7), impacted every phase of life in the church. Understandably, early Christian positions on social issues were greatly modified by the belief that life as they knew it would soon come to an end. Slavery, Roman oppression, taxes, marriages, economic inequities, persecution: These and all conditions and relationships were soon to end and a new world would dawn. With the passing of time, the experience of the delay of Christ's return created both theological and practical problems for the church, as we shall see in 2 Peter. The New Testament itself reflects a number of attempts to warn those too much motivated by end-of-the-world thinking that quality of life and attention to ministry and mission are not to collapse simply because of "the delay" (note especially Matthew 24—25 and Mark 13). The operative advice is: Continue your work, remain responsible, be awake and alert, and be serious (Greek, "sober," v. 7) about your conduct and relationships (1 Thess. 5:6; Mark 13:32–37).

The attitudes and patterns of behavior that constitute living by the will of God are four in number. First is the disciplined life of prayer (v. 7). A consistent prayer life, that is, one which is not activated only in crisis, requires preparation, exercising faculties of mind, heart, will, and soul. Who can pray for others without knowing them and their circumstances? Who can pray for oneself without thoughtful self-examination and reflection? And who can pray at all without searching for the mind and will of God? No wonder Jesus' disciples asked "Lord, teach us to pray" (Luke 11:1). No wonder Paul acknowledged, "We do not know how to pray as we ought, but that very Spirit intercedes with sighs too deep for words" (Rom. 8:26). Even with our own best efforts, we rely on the Spirit because the Spirit knows the will of God.

Second, turn toward each other in constant mutual love (v. 8). Just as the prayer life is one of discipline, so the life of love for each other must be constant, that is, strenuous and intense. Otherwise the Christian fellowship can be sabotaged by the mood swings of a few members or petty grudges of others. The proverb, "love covers a multitude of sins" (see also James 5:20) is most appropriate in every congregation. Not every emotional and psychic bruise can be given attention; otherwise all the church's energy for mission and witness would be burned up in damage control. The atmosphere of constant love and mutual forgiveness heals as well as prevents those tensions that occur in every family but that are not fatal to the fellowship.

Third, practice hospitality ungrudgingly and without complaining (v. 9). The word "hospitality" means literally "love of strangers." In one sense the practice was essential to the life of the church because traveling teachers, prophets, and evangelists depended on the hospitality of the saints in order to carry out their mission (Heb. 13:1–2; 3 John 5–8). Of course, there were abuses by those who preyed on the churches. The early Christian document called the *Didache* deals at length with the problem in chapters 11–12. But even so, hospitality continued for centuries as a hallmark of Christianity. The reason for it lay deeper than practical necessity. Jesus had spoken often of both the giving and receiving of hospitality. When his disciples went out on missions, they were dependent on the hospitality of those to whom they were sent (Luke 10:1–12), and Jesus praised those who welcomed strangers (Matt. 10:40–42). In fact, he elevated hospitality to strangers as one of the criteria for entering finally into the joy of the Lord (Matt. 25:31–46). But the practice already had a history long before Jesus. "The alien who resides with you shall be to you as the citizen among you; you shall love the alien as yourself, for you were aliens in the land of Egypt" (Lev. 19:34). Take a moment to reflect on the remarkable nature of this expectation of hospitable behavior on the part of God's people toward strangers. Ordinarily one would expect the recollection of one's own painful past to motivate revenge, or getting even, or passing on unwittingly to the next generation the abuse once endured in one's own life. Is that not the way it works in marriages, in families, in societies? Not among God's people. The memory of their own experience was to generate the empathy essential to genuine hospitality. It is worth noting that the root of our word "hospitality," *hospes*, originally meant both host and guest. The implication seems to be that whenever two or more are fellowshiping and it is not discernible who is host and who is guest, then hospitality is being practiced.

Finally, living by the will of God means using the gifts God has granted in service to the common good (vv. 10–11). The word for "gift," *charisma*, does not refer to physical attractiveness or magnetic personality ("I know he will be elected; he has charisma") but to some spiritual gift God has provided each member of the fellowship. Since each one has a gift (v. 10), then everyone is a charismatic; that is, each one has been equipped to serve. Paul spoke of many gifts (1 Corinthians 12; Rom. 12:3–8), but here only two are mentioned: speaking the word of God and serving. The word "serving" is a general one, perhaps used deliberately to say that the form of service is determined by the needs of the other.

The discussion of gifts here sounds very much like Rom. 12:3–8. Two emphases are quite clear: First, gifts are not for flaunting or appearing superior but for service. Speaking the word *seems* superior to waiting tables but, in fact, it is not. For a charisma to be used to distance one from another contradicts the meaning of charisma: a gift from God. Second, the household or family of God and not the individual is the primary category for thinking about gifts. We have already observed more than once that these Christians are aliens in the world, but they are members of the household of God. To be a responsible member of the household is to be a steward of everything committed into one's care. No one in the household is so gifted as to have no family chores. Perhaps "chores" sounds too burdensome, too boring, too menial for a description of life and work in the household of God, and so it would be if our service did not begin and end with doxology. It is to God's service we have been called, and all our words and work are to God's glory. To God alone belong all praise and authority, in this life and in the life to come.

As Christ's Partners in Both Suffering and Glory (1 Peter 4:12–19)

4:12 **Beloved, do not be surprised at the fiery ordeal that is taking place among you to test you, as though something strange were happening to you.** [13] **But rejoice insofar as you are sharing Christ's sufferings, so that you may also be glad and shout for joy when his glory is revealed.** [14] **If you are reviled for the name of Christ, you are blessed, because the spirit of glory, which is the Spirit of God, is resting on you.** [15] **But let none of you suffer as a murderer, a thief, a criminal, or even as a mischief maker.** [16] **Yet if any of you suffers as a Christian, do not consider it a disgrace, but glorify God because you bear this name.** [17] **For the time has come for judgment to begin with the household of God; if it begins with us, what will be the end for those who do not obey the gospel of God?** [18] **And**
  "If it is hard for the righteous to be saved,
      what will become of the ungodly and the sinners?"
[19] **Therefore, let those suffering in accordance with God's will entrust themselves to a faithful Creator, while continuing to do good.**

In this unit we return to the theme of suffering, but we do not have mere repetition; several interpretations of suffering are here either developed further or are entirely new.

However, before discussing the message of this passage, a word needs to be said about what appears to be a radical break between verses 11 and 12. The reader experiences a shift and the NRSV marks that fact by triple spacing before beginning 4:12.

There are several literary signals to indicate that 4:11 is an ending and 4:12 is a beginning. A doxology rounds off the discussion concluding at 4:11 and the "Amen" sounds like the end of a letter. Verse 12 begins with "Beloved," a word of address that appears to be the beginning of a letter. In addition, the sudden introduction of a "fiery ordeal," which may have surprised some of the believers, seems much more intense than the suffering previously discussed in the letter. A number of theories have been put forward to account for this noticeable disjuncture. Perhaps 1:1–4:11 was a baptismal liturgy or homily and 4:12 begins the letter proper. One popular theory is that 1:1–4:11 preceded baptism and 4:12–5:14 followed baptism. In other words, the spacing in the NRSV represents the point of the act of baptism. Others have guessed that 4:12–5:14 is the work of a different hand, perhaps a later addition. One interesting speculation is that in the process of writing the letter, the author received news of an outbreak of severe persecution against Christians in Asia Minor and penned an additional message noting that fact and offering stronger encouragement.

Any one of these theories may represent what was in fact the case, but we should also point out that none of them are necessary to explain the transition at 4:12. First, recall that doxologies and even "Amen" can be found sprinkled through letters at points clearly not ending those letters. As examples, look at Rom. 1:25; 9:5; 11:36; Gal. 1:5; Eph. 3:21; 1 Thess. 3:13, and even later in this letter (5:11). As for "Beloved" appearing to be an introductory word, the writer has earlier used this term of address at 2:11 (see also 1 Cor. 10:14; Rom. 12:19). And to say that "fiery ordeal" is a new subject or a reference to suffering different in kind and intensity from that discussed earlier is to overlook several clues in the letter itself. The writer has already referred to the readers' experiences as being a test of fire, analogous to that used to purify and to test metals (1:6–7). The image is one familiar to readers of the Old Testament (Psalm 66:10; Prov. 27:21; Mal. 3:1–3). There is no reason supplied either by the text or by history to assume the reference to a test by fire indicates Roman persecution by incendiarism. We have no evidence that at this early date Romans torched Christians in Asia Minor as the mad Nero had done in Rome in his effort to shift from himself the blame for burning the city.

There is another sense in which "fiery ordeal" is appropriate here. It is the language of eschatology (that is, the doctrine of the end time), and this passage clearly asserts "the time has come" (v. 17; also earlier at v. 7). To be sure, the end time when Christ's glory is revealed (v. 13) will be, even for God's people, a distressing time. In fact, judgment will begin with the household of God (v. 17). There is nothing here of rapturous exemption for the saints as some arrogant bumper stickers announce ("In case of rapture, you may have this car"). Quite the contrary, the lives and works of Christians must stand up under judgment (Mark 13:9–13; Rom. 13:11–14; 1 Cor. 11:32) and be proven by fire (Mal. 3:1–6; 1 Cor. 3:12–15). Judgment is an element of salvation, and those who remain faithful to the end will "be glad and shout for joy" (v. 13). In short, the fiery present is a sign that this age is near an end and the birth pangs of the new are beginning. So, said Jesus, "Stand up and raise your heads, because your redemption is drawing near" (Luke 21:28).

And so, the reader should not be surprised by verse 12 just as the Christians of Asia Minor should not have been surprised by the fiery ordeal among them. Suffering was part of the Christian vocation. Jesus had said so (Mark 13:9–13) and the early missionaries were quite up front about it. As Paul reminded the church at Thessalonica, "When we were with you, we told you beforehand that we were to suffer persecution; so it turned out, as you know" (1 Thess. 3:4). Gospels of painless success and uninterrupted smiles have, of course been preached. They still are. Turn on the TV and some preacher will offer Jesus as the way to be healthy, wealthy, and wise. But the history of faithfulness in work and witness says such a promise is simple, shallow, deceptive, and productive of guilt feelings in sincere Christians whose faith meets pain and opposition. On a deeper level, however, there is profound joy (v. 13), not because of special exemption from affliction but because one has been admitted to the circle of those who share the sufferings of Christ. This does not mean that "if you really are Christian" you will go grinning through Gethsemane. The sharing (or fellowship, v. 13) of Christ's suffering is the sharing of his ministry of love, forgiveness, embrace of the marginalized, and his call for equal justice for all people, a ministry that then and now brings opposition from vested interests and threatened prejudices. In other words, the fellowship of Christ's suffering (see also Rom. 8:17; Phil. 3:10; 2 Tim. 2:11–12) is not joined at the time of suffering; it is joined at the time of service and witness, and the suffering follows. The suffering at the hands of the critical and abusive culture was interpreted by the church as evidence that they were being faithful to the will of God as it had been lived out by Jesus Christ. It was this understanding that gave them joy (Acts 5:41). Of course, to suffer because one has violated the law or been involved in mischief (v. 15, "meddling in the affairs of others") is to lose the joy and the blessing. Suffering in itself is neither a badge of honor nor a mark of disgrace. The sufferer has to ask, What did I do right? as well as, What did I do wrong?

Being "reviled for the name of Christ" (v. 14) not only echoes a teaching of Jesus (Matt. 5:11; Mark 13:13) but brings up the interesting yet difficult question of whether bearing the name of Christ was in itself an offense. It seems clear from the passage that being identified as a Christian was itself enough to draw verbal abuse and social isolation. Whether the word "Christian" was at this time and place a slur or nickname is not clear, either here (v. 16) or in the two other appearances of the word in the New Testament (Acts 11:26; 26:28). We do know that early in the second century followers of Jesus wore the name as a self-designation. In the late second and early third centuries Christian writers were urging governmental authorities not to judge a person solely on the basis of the name but to examine the person's conduct and quality of life. That the government had probably not entered the picture as persecutor of Christians as early as 1 Peter did not remove the hurt and fear that society can inflict without legal warrant. What's in a name? is no inconsequential question. During the two World Wars, loyal Americans whose names reflected a German background were maligned, intimidated, suspected, and shunned. In World War II thousands of Japanese Americans were detained in compounds, not because of conduct but because of the name. Protestant America, not many years ago, questioned whether John Kennedy was qualified for the presidency because he was Catholic. And even today, expressions such as "the new neighbors are black" or "his boss is a Jew" or "that church has a woman minister" activate in many quarters old stereotypes and prejudices, totally apart from any knowledge of conduct or performance. So it must have been in Asia Minor: "They tell me some Christians have moved in across the street," or "My daughter says there is a Christian enrolled at her school," or "I'll not shop there as long as it's run by Christians."

The writer understands how difficult it is to remain faithful, how easy it is to quit. But, he says, the end is near and God's judgment will be on us as well as on the ungodly. Do not, however, fear that judgment, for that day will reveal God's glory and in that you will share. Do not be paralyzed by intimidation but continue in good works. And if you join Christ in suffering, join him also in putting your trust in the faithful Creator, for Christ, in both life and death, was able to say, "Father, into your hands I commend my spirit" (Luke 23:46; also earlier in this letter at 2:23).

The Elders Bear Special Responsibility
(1 Peter 5:1–5a)

5:1 **Now as an elder myself and a witness of the sufferings of Christ, as well as one who shares in the glory to be revealed, I exhort the elders among you** [2] **to tend the flock of God that is in your charge, exercising the oversight, not under compulsion but willingly, as God would have you do it—not for sordid gain but eagerly.** [3] **Do not lord it over those in your charge, but be**

examples to the flock. ⁴ And when the chief shepherd appears, you will win the crown of glory that never fades away. ⁵ In the same way, you who are younger must accept the authority of the elders.

This exhortation to the leadership of the churches is brief but extremely important. The already difficult situation of the young congregations (probably house churches) would have been precarious, if not fatal, without strong leadership. In a later generation during a period of severe persecution, Polycarp, bishop of Smyrna (a city on the west coast of Asia Minor) wanted to die a martyr for Christ. He was, however, persuaded to hide out because his leadership was needed even more during those trying times. The conditions described in 1 Peter, though short of martyrdom, made the burdens of leadership especially heavy. And it is important to notice that the message to the leaders is not penned to them in a separate note but in the letter to all the church. When the letter was read to the whole assembly, the elders received their message with everyone listening; there could be no confusion about leadership and respect for leadership.

Two questions more of historical interest than theological importance are prompted by these verses: Who is the one writing as a fellow elder, and who are elders anyway? As for the first question, it is possible to read "a witness of the sufferings of Christ" (5:1) as indicating that the writer actually saw the crucifixion. This would imply one of the circle of Jesus' friends, and in light of 1:1, Simon Peter himself. However, this need not be the meaning of the phrase. A witness is not necessarily an eyewitness but one who testifies to one's faith by word and life. The writer could be saying that he joins the reader in the sufferings of Christ and is not hesitant so to testify. In fact, 5:1 seems parallel to 4:13: All of us share in the suffering and will share in the glory to be revealed. Those who argue for Petrine authorship also point out that the charge to tend the flock recalls Christ's words to Peter to tend and to feed the flock (John 21:15–17), but the language here is more nearly that of Paul's charge to the elders of the church in Ephesus (Acts 20:17–35), a city also in Asia Minor: Care for the flock, exercise oversight, and beware of the love of money. And finally, being a fellow elder does not fit comfortably with being an apostle (1:1). At least the evidence of the New Testament points to a clear distinction between apostles and elders (Acts 15:2, 6, 23; 21:18; Titus 1:5).

It is possible, then, to understand "as an elder myself and a witness of the sufferings of Christ" as the signature of an anonymous church leader who is within the circle of Peter's influence, perhaps his disciple, and writing in Peter's name (1:1). As indicated earlier, however, one's interpretation of the phrase neither adds nor subtracts materially when we listen to the message itself. We have paused here simply because we relish every word that may contribute to our effort to see more clearly through the window of the early church. Desire to know the quarry from which we are hewn is not idle curiosity.

As for the second question, Who is an elder? we proceed with a bit more clarity. The word itself, *presbyter*, means "one who is older" and hence, according to widespread belief, "one who is wiser." This wisdom, joined to the respect accorded the older members of a community, made for an easy move from "older" to "leader." Judaism provided a background of leadership by elders (Exod. 18:13–27; Num. 11:16–30; Matt. 15:2; Mark 14:43; Luke 7:3), and it would be natural for the early church so to structure itself (Acts 15:2; 21:18; Titus 1:5; James 5:14). We cannot say for sure that every congregation had a number of elders; very likely there were varieties of ecclesiastical structures just as there are today. In the New Testament the word "elder" never lost totally its primary sense of older person (1 Tim. 5:1; Philemon 9) and very likely some of that sense is preserved here since the exhortation to elders is followed by advice to "you who are younger" (v. 5). The younger were not a leadership group but did represent a pocket of power sometimes poised to replace older and perhaps more cautious and conservative leadership. In 1 Timothy, list of duties included advice to younger and older members (5:1–16). Although Jesus himself ran afoul of the elders of his community, the New Testament generally affirms the seasoned leadership of older members. Later, a leader of the church in Rome named Clement wrote a letter to the church in Corinth chastising the younger members for revolting against the older. But sometimes the health of the church demands such a change in leadership, even if painfully done.

The elders, then, are to be shepherds of the flock, taking their cue from the chief shepherd (v. 4; John 10:1–16). The task is pastoral, involving care; it is educational, involving nurture and feeding; it is administrative, involving oversight. The leader does not perform as one who, having been lashed, now lashes others, but rather as one who accepts the role willingly and cheerfully (vv. 2–3). Sometimes persons rise to places of leadership in the church when they could not do so in any other arena. This fact can be a compliment to the church that provides resources and support without prejudice and without the cutthroat competition one finds elsewhere. But the same fact must alert the church to the possibility of arrogance, browbeating, and intimidation by persons who lead in church but nowhere else.

Leadership, and especially sudden leadership, can bring out the worst as well as the best in a person. And nowhere is this more evident than in the area of financial gain. At least in some churches the elders were paid (1 Tim. 5:17–18), and the prospect of material gain no doubt attracted the unqualified (Rom. 16:18; Phil. 3:17–19). To prevent even a rumor of such a violation of church leadership, Paul reminded the Ephesian elders that he had done manual labor to support his mission among them (Acts 20:33–35). But not even the haunting figure of Judas and the repulsive ring of thirty pieces of silver tossed on the temple floor could protect the church from hirelings who saw the flock as so much fleece and flesh. Perhaps financial carelessness breeds in a room where love, forgiveness, and trust overflow. Or it may be that greed is not as present in the church as elsewhere, but we are more aware of it because it is such a contradiction to the life of Jesus and of his call to discipleship. Whatever the reasons, and whatever the circumstances in Asia Minor, the writer felt the need to say to the church leaders what they already knew: "not for sordid gain" (v. 2).

A Closing Exhortation to All (1 Peter 5:5b–11)

5:5b **And all of you most clothe yourself with humility in your dealings with one another, for**

> **"God opposes the proud,**
> > **but gives grace to the humble."**

⁶ Humble yourselves therefore under the mighty hand of God, so that he may exalt you in due time. ⁷ Cast all your anxiety on him, because he cares for you. ⁸ Discipline yourselves, keep alert. Like a roaring lion your adversary the devil prowls around, looking for someone to devour. ⁹ Resist him, steadfast in your faith, for you know that your brothers and sisters in all the world are undergoing the same kinds of suffering. ¹⁰ And after you have suffered for a little while, the God of all grace, who has called you to his eternal glory in Christ, will himself restore, support, strengthen, and establish you. ¹¹ To him be the power forever and ever. Amen.

You probably recall that earlier in this letter the writer turned from addressing specific groups (slaves, wives, husbands) to speak to everyone (2:18–3:8). So here, instructions to elders and younger members are followed by "And all of you must" (v. 5). And in each case the subject matter is not changed but is rather enlarged to apply to all. And why not? In any community in which there is a great distance between the quality of life for the leaders and for the general membership, problems erupt. What follows, therefore, is a series of exhortations that have no integral relation to each other but all of which concern life that is lived before a God who exalts the humble, cares for the anxious, and ultimately will "restore, support, strengthen, and establish you" (v. 10). These exhortations are in the form of a series of proverbs, one of which is quoted from Prov. 3:34. Proverbs are brief, pithy sayings of wisdom, distilled from experience, and easy to remember, an important feature for an oral culture. Given the common nature of human experience, proverbs are highly portable and of universal application. The Gospels record more than one hundred proverbs from the lips of Jesus ("physician, heal yourself"; "a city set on a hill cannot be hid"; "do not cast pearls before swine"; etc.) and the epistle of James is often called the book of Christian wisdom.

As with most proverbs, the sayings here require little if any elaboration. Humility should mark the relationship of the members to each other as well as their relationship to God. To "clothe yourselves with humility" may present the image of putting on the apron or work frock of the servant. As Paul expressed the same thought, "Do nothing from selfish ambition or conceit, but in humility regard others as better than yourselves" (Phil. 2:3). This was, he said, the mind of Christ. Whatever exalting is to be done will not be self-exaltation but the ac t of God "in due time"; that is, in God's own time (see Matt. 23:12; James 4:6). But even now God cares what happens to the church. There is no need to try to hide one's anxieties about church and family and self as though such worries were evidence of no faith. A small, new congregation in a hostile environment was a condition that spawned anxieties. Rather than whistle in the dark, pretending they are not there, open up, express the fears, and lay them in the lap of God. Not that one goes home from such a prayer service forever free of problems. The disciplines of work, witness, and prayer cannot for an hour be abandoned. (This is now the third time that the writer has urged discipline; see 1:13; 4:7; 5:8.) Constant vigilance is necessary in order to discern what is *really* going on behind what is going on. This is to say, the writer subscribes to the view commonly held at the time that back of the acts of evil in the world stood the devil, the adversary of all good, the perverter of God's efforts to redeem the world. This demonic force inspired those who killed Jesus (1 Cor. 2:8), and all who are engaged in evil activity are "following the ruler of the power of the air, the spirit that is now at work among those who are disobedient" (Eph. 2:2). We had occasion to consider these powers of evil in the commentary on 3:22. The difference here is that evil is in 5:8 personified in a single figure whose goal is to destroy the faith of God's people. To succumb to harassment and abuse is to fall victim to the chief engineer of evil and to die spiritually. This, says the writer, is what is really going on. This is what Christians are up against. "For our struggle is not against enemies of blood and flesh, but against the rulers, against the authorities, against the cosmic powers of this present darkness, against the spiritual forces of evil in the heavenly places" (Eph. 6:12).

In view of the fact that this language and worldview are different from that of most moderns, several comments are in order. First, it is not sufficient for us to state what we do *not* believe. The point is, what *do* we believe about evil and good in the world? How do we account for such gross violence and inhumanity still raging in our time? We are as hard pressed as were our forebears in the attempt to understand much that is going on. Saying "I do not believe in a devil" has not diminished evil in the world. Second, God is not aloof from the fray, but in the person of Jesus has entered into the pain and ambiguity of life. Third, we believe that the apparent defeat of God at the crucifixion has been reversed at the empty tomb. Life wins out over death and this conviction will be vindicated in the final revelation of God's power and glory. And finally, the "in the meantime" life of faith calls for both vigilance and discernment. While evil sometimes erupts as violence and cruelty, evil also works in disguise, insinuating itself into the circles of the well-intentioned. If Jesus could look at a close friend and say, "Get behind me, Satan!" why should I assume all is well just because no horns and pitchforks are in sight?

No words to suffering saints are totally healing but the writer does offer two helpful reminders. One, you are not alone in your distress; your brothers and sisters everywhere are experiencing what you are now facing. Two, this suffering is not going to continue endlessly. After "a little while" (admittedly, time moves slowly for those in pain) you will share in the final triumph of God. The God of grace who called you to be a church will attend personally to all your needs. That very thought, the keen anticipation of that finale, again evokes a burst of praise (v. 11).

It is not insignificant that the body of the letter concludes with the praise of God; with the worship of God the letter began (1:3–12) and along the way the writer paused to sing (4:11). To sprinkle the narrative of God's activity in the world with bits of liturgy is the way of the Bible, a tradition that still survives among many black and some white congregations. These moments of praise are not interruptions but stirring reminders of the presence and immediate availability of God. All talk about God must arise from and return to talk with God; otherwise the finest eloquence is but a noisy gong. But every congregation will listen attentively to the sermon that has an altar in it.

GREETINGS
1 Peter 5:12–14a

5:12 **Through Silvanus, whom I consider a faithful brother, I have written this short letter to encourage you and to testify that this is the true grace of God. Stand fast in it.** [13] **Your sister church in Babylon, chosen together with you, sends you greetings; and so does my son Mark.** [14] **Greet one another with a kiss of love.**

In keeping with the customary epistolary form, 1 Peter concludes with greetings and farewell. Ordinarily the greetings were brief, consisting of a personal word from the writer, any immediate associates of the writer known to the addressees, and any others whose names might give weight of credibility to the writer. Paul tended to mention his fellow workers and sometimes quite a few others if he were writing to a church to which he was not personally known (compare Romans 16 and Colossians 4). In the present case two names join that of the author as well as of the entire church in Rome (Babylon), presumably the place of the letter's origin. Silvanus, Mark, and the church in "Babylon" were discussed in the introduction to this letter and that material need not be repeated here. What may bear repeating, however, is the fact that this is not a private letter. It is not only to churches in Asia Minor but it is from a church. Granted, the signature is that of Peter, an apostle of Jesus Christ, but joining Peter are a faithful brother, a son in the faith, and a sister church. A few scholars have argued that "your sister church" wrongly translates "she who is your fellow elected one" and that the phrase really refers to Peter's wife (1 Cor. 9:5). However, the same expression clearly refers to the church in 2 John 1, 13 and most likely does here as well. Given the fact that the governing image in the letter is the household of God (although in the world you are exiles and aliens), these terms of greeting: a fellow elder, a brother, a son, a sister, were especially warm, without appearance of superiority, and quite likely well received. Equally appropriate is the admonition not only to receive these greetings from distant brothers and sisters but to use the occasion of the letter to greet each other with the kiss of love. Such an act would not only heal any wounds that might have been opened by the letter but would also remind the receiving church that they had each other and that mutual love was the stuff of church, apostle or no apostle, letter or no letter, Rome or no Rome. The practice of sharing a holy kiss, familiar in Paul's churches and known to have been a part of worship in Syrian churches generations after Paul, apparently died out soon after. Perhaps the reason lay in the public charge that Christians practiced free love.

Unlike the closing greetings in many letters, 1 Peter contains here a brief statement of the writer's purpose. This brief letter, he says, is to encourage the readers, and he has done that; to testify to the true grace of God, and he has done that; and to urge them to stand firm in that grace, and he has done that. The message is finished, greetings have been shared; there remains only the benediction.

FAREWELL
1 Peter 5:14b

5:14b **Peace to all of you who are in Christ.**

The final word is a benediction. Paul likewise closed with a benediction but with him the last word was usually "The grace of our Lord Jesus Christ be with you" (1 Thess. 5:28). Both 1 Peter and Paul speak of grace and peace in the salutation, but at the end, Paul repeats grace. Here the writer has repeated the word of grace in the greetings (v. 12) but his very, very last word is peace, shalom. For Paul whose own faith struggle and whose message centered always on how God deals with sinners, grace had to be the last word spoken, the last word heard. But given the conditions in Asia Minor under which these Christians labored to remain faithful, the last word to be spoken, the last word to be heard had to be peace. No other benediction could send them home quite so well.

A FINAL WORD

Permit me a closing suggestion. Now that we have walked together through 1 Peter, return to the introduction and read it again. The reasons I think this might be helpful are two. First, I said at the outset that much of what is said in introductions to books is really of the nature of conclusions. The commentator writes as one who has already studied the text but in many cases the reader has not. Perhaps now that this study of 1 Peter is finished, the introduction will be more clear and more helpful. The second reason is that attention to the details within the units and subunits of the text tend to rob us of the memory of the document as a whole. Reading again the introduction can help restore one's sense of the overall message of the book and that, after all, is what we want to hear.

Second Peter

Introduction

In my brief introduction to these three epistles a few comments were made about 2 Peter that you may wish to review before we proceed further. What was not said there, however, is that this epistle is seldom read and studied even less. Pulpits point parishioners to the grand narratives of the Old Testament, to the songs and oracles of Israel, to the Gospels, Acts, and Paul, but who has urged us to drink of the wisdom of 2 Peter lest we die? In the Revised Common Lectionary, readings from this letter occur only twice. Preachers seem more willing to lead their listeners into the terrible splendor of Revelation than into the unfamiliar world of this brief message "to those who have received a faith as precious as ours" (1:1). How are we to understand this neglect by the very church that has embraced 2 Peter as a document of Christian scripture?

Those of a practical turn with no interest in the theological merits or demerits of a piece of literature simply remind us that 2 Peter is a small book and tucked away near the back of the New Testament. In a Bible of 1,084 pages, this letter occupies less than 3. This observation is pertinent but only a partial answer. Some complain of its style—elaborate, ornate, and grandiose—as though it is hesitant to share its message with just anybody. The vocabulary is unusual (55 words appear nowhere else in the New Testament), sentences are long, and natural breaks in thought are few. Still others consider the content as less worthy of the church's attention than most of the other writings of the New Testament. Much like the even briefer Jude, 2 Peter engages in quite a bit of name calling. Granted, the writer is vigorously involved in a battle with certain persons in the church who are regarded as both wrong and dangerous to the community of faith, but many modern readers tend to think of such heretics as long dead, or off somewhere in their own denomination, or to be tolerated in a church that shrugs its shoulders over most doctrinal disputes anyway. Should we, then, think of 2 Peter as a historical marker where we should pause, recall ancient battles fought for the faith, express gratitude for the progress we have made, and move on?

Not yet. It is true that much dispute has arisen over the quality and relevance of the message of 2 Peter. Words such as "unpleasant," "dubious," "embarrassing," and "stepchild" have been written by persons no less committed to the gospel of Christ than the rest of us. In the early days of the church, heavy and prayerful discussions attended to the many Christian writings available to the believers in efforts to discern which were inspired of God and deserving of a place in the church's canon. About the great majority of the books in our New Testament there was little or no dispute, but 2 Peter was on that short list under the heading "Writings Spoken Against." Even so, the epistle survived the debate and took its place among those documents that together provide the normative guide for the faith and life of the Christian community. It is with this respect and willingness to listen that I introduce this letter, using the same format that served to introduce 1 Peter.

WHAT WE ALREADY KNOW

From the comments above, one would assume that the reader of 2 Peter would come upon no familiar person, place, phrase, or idea. But even though most Christians are not very knowledgeable about book, chapter, and verse, and even though sermons and lessons on 2 Peter are few and far between, some bits and pieces have filtered into our common culture and lie at the dim edges of memory. To identify those items and associate them with 2 Peter will help us relax and listen.

Of the persons mentioned in the letter there are six whom we have met before. First and foremost is Jesus Christ, the center of the author's faith and ours. Then there is the person whose signature opens the letter: "Simeon Peter, a servant and apostle of Jesus Christ." We know him as Simon Peter, however, the more Hebraic Simeon occurring only one other time in the New Testament (Acts 15:14). And, of course, we know Paul (3:15). However, "our beloved brother Paul" does not sound familiar to those who remember the tension between Peter and Paul in the church at Antioch in Syria (Gal. 2:11–14). Perhaps reconciliation had taken place. We meet again from the Old Testament Noah and Lot (2:5–8), two classic examples of God's power and willingness to rescue the righteous from grossly evil circumstances (Genesis 6—8; 19). These two had already found a place together in early Christian preaching (Luke 17:26–32). And finally there is Balaam, the prophet who loved money more than truth. He is less familiar in Christian circles and probably would not be remembered at all had not his own jackass rebuked him for his transgression (2:15–16; Numbers 22). It helps when entering a strange room to see a few faces we recognize. We have grown so accustomed, however, to Paul's habit of introducing his co-workers and saying Hello to significant persons among the addressees that we miss that personal touch here. Silence in this matter may have been justified or necessary in 2 Peter, but it does not help the reader feel comfortably at home.

As for places that might be familiar, we are even less fortunate. Only Sodom and Gomorrah (2:6) are mentioned and that reference is the usual one: those ancient cities, known for their inhospitality and sexual perversity (Gen. 19:1–11), were destroyed as examples of God's judgment on the wicked. They have maintained that notoriety in Jewish and Christian preaching to this day (Deut. 29:16–28; Ezek. 16:46–50; Amos 4:11; Matt. 10:15; Luke 10:12; Rom. 9:29). But the most important questions of place remain unanswered: Where is the writer? Where are the readers?

When we come to the question, What ideas, concepts, or events in 2 Peter are already known? the first-time reader is in for a pleasant surprise. The transfiguration of Jesus, one of the most familiar stories in the Gospels (Matt. 17:1–8; Mark 9:2–8; Luke 9:28–36) is mentioned only once in the New Testament outside the Gospels: in 2 Peter 1:17–18. Some readers may recall that Jesus predicted Simon Peter would die a martyr (John 21:18), a prediction repeated here at 1:14. We meet here also two fairly familiar sayings of Jesus: (1) that he will "come like a thief" (3:10; in the night, Matt. 24:43; 1 Thess. 5:2) and (2) that of backsliders it can be said, "the last state has become worse for them than the first" (2:20; Matt. 12:45; Luke 11:26). And who has not heard, "With the Lord one day is like a thousand years, and a thousand years are like one day" (3:8)? A popular Christian hymn sings of Christ as "the bright and morning star," although memory here may draw more from Rev. 22:16 than 2 Peter 1:19. And from countless sermons will be recalled the sentiment if not the words of 3:9: "The Lord . . . is patient with you, not wanting any to perish, but all to come to repentance." One does not even have to be a churchgoer to hear talk to the effect that the world once destroyed by water will be destroyed by fire next time (3:7, 10, 12), following which there will be "new heavens and a new earth" (3:13). Less familiar except to those attracted to sermons on "The Unpardonable Sin" and "Will We Get a Second Chance?" is the grim announcement of 2:21: "For it would have been better for them never to have known the way of righteousness than, after knowing it, to turn back from the holy commandment that was passed on to them." And finally, a few readers may be sufficiently at home in apocalyptic literature to recognize in the casting down of angels from heaven into hell (2:4), a very ancient theme in both Judaism and Christianity (Gen. 6:1–4; Rev. 12:7–9), a theme dramatically developed in John Milton's *Paradise Lost*. All in all, for the one entering this epistle for the first time, at least with this level of seriousness, enough recognition has occurred to awaken further curiosity and to make the exercise ahead of us less daunting.

WHAT WE WISH TO KNOW

All of us have our own questions when we read a text, but of a text in the New Testament we have at least one primary question in common: Does this writing yield a portrait of Jesus Christ, and if so, who is he? For example, 1 Peter presented Jesus Christ not only as crucified, raised, and coming again but also as one whose suffering and response to abuse was an example for us all. Here in 2 Peter, however, the Christ we meet is a glorious one. He is referred to as "our Lord and Savior Jesus Christ" (1:1–2, 11; 2:20; 3:2, 18) who will come again in judgment (3:4–10).

It may be that in 1:1 Christ is called God, rare indeed in the New Testament (John 20:28; Rom. 9:5; Titus 2:13; Heb. 1:8–9). In a very broad statement, Christ is said to have joined the prophets before him and the apostles after him in passing along the true tradition (3:2). The one event from the life of Jesus given specific attention is the transfiguration (1:17–18), a presentation of him as the heavenly and glorious one. The letter is silent about his suffering and crucifixion. There is a reference to "the Master who bought them" in 2:1, which could allude to the death of Jesus as a ransom, but this is not likely the meaning. The subject matter in which this phrase occurs concerns false prophets whose preaching is for sale and if someone offers more than Christ, they take the highest bid.

Second Peter does not offer a Christ whose life is for us a model nor one with whom we can identify in our suffering. He is our Savior, by which title the writer means that Christ's divine power and goodness make it possible for us to become "participants of the divine nature" (1:4). That realm generally spoken of as "the kingdom of God" is here "the eternal kingdom of our Lord and Savior Jesus Christ" (1:11). The frequent urging that believers grow in the knowledge of Jesus Christ is not biographical or historical in its intent; the expression is interchangeable with the knowledge of God. We cannot, of course, know how much of the earthly career of Jesus was known to the readers. The writer has specific problems to address and perhaps references to material we have in the Gospels simply do not serve that purpose. We do know the writer assumed the readers knew *the* or *a* Christian tradition: "Therefore, I intend to keep on reminding you of these things, though you know them already and are established in the truth that has come to you" (1:12).

This leads us to ask about the relationship of the writer to the readers. When the author seeks "to refresh your memory" (1:13), does this mean theirs is a relationship of long standing, the writer having been to the readers the one who passed along to them the apostolic tradition? Perhaps, but it could be that they are being reminded of that instruction all Christians received. The author does say, "This is now, beloved, the second letter I am writing to you" (3:1), but as we shall see, neither the situation of the readers of 1 Peter nor the message of that letter seems to have any continuity with 2 Peter. If there was or is a relationship between writer and readers, it is concealed from us. There are no greetings from anyone to anyone. The signature is formal and the recipients are addressed in a most general way (1:1). There is no farewell and the repeated use of "beloved" was a not uncommon literary device that did not necessarily sustain or initiate a personal relationship.

Who, then, are these recipients? The writer may have known, but we do not. To us they are "those who have received faith as precious as ours through the righteousness of our God and Savior Jesus Christ" (1:1). It is possible, of course, that a specific church was the destination and the relation between the writer and readers was such that no further identification was necessary. However, lacking evidence of that circumstance, the church has placed 2 Peter among the general or catholic epistles, and with no mention of even a broad geographical area, this letter is even more general than 1 Peter. In other words, this is a letter to Christians, whatever the address. Given some kinship between the heresy being combatted and the heresies known to have flourished in Asia Minor, some have assigned the letter to that area, but that is only a guess. Since the author considers his words to have lasting value beyond his own lifetime (1:15), there seems to be a conscious effort to present timeless truth. The readers seem to be Gentiles. Even though the Old Testament provides warnings, the holy prophets are presented as authoritative voices, and at least one text of Jewish scripture is cited (Prov. 26:11), this represents no more (less, in fact) than a Gentile Christian community would know and accept. Given the strong Hellenistic flavor in the images and terminology (for ex-

ample, hell is neither Sheol nor Gehenna but Tartarus, a Greek name for
the place of punishment for the dead), the Christians addressed here are
familiar with and probably have absorbed much of the culture into their
faith. We know from our own situations as well as from history that some
translation of the faith into a culture's categories and vocabulary is not
only inevitable but necessary if the faith is to be indigenous and relevant.
The issue is one of degree. The gospel loses meaning when the old
phrases, however antiquarian and meaningless, are simply repeated. On
the other hand, are the updates and modern equivalents really equivalent?
When passing from one country to another, old money is exchanged for
new, but one often wonders whether value is lost in the process. So with
the passing along of the gospel. The writer of 2 Peter feels strongly that
something has been lost in the translation. To that concern we will attend
later.

Finally, we wish to know what it is to be Christian in the time and place
of this document. There is a sense in which this is an unfair question to
ask of any text not written to answer it. But within the constraints of a
writer's purpose and primary subject matter, there still is revealed in a letter of a Christian leader to a church what is particularly vital to being the
church in that place and what characteristics of the Christian life need un-
derscoring. One finds here what is expected of any such writing: calls for
sincerity, steadfastness, godly living, and growth in faith and character.
However, the lessons that the letter most frequently urges upon the reader
both answer and ask what it is to be Christian in that circumstance. The
primary lessons are three: One, to be Christian is to know the Lord. But
then we must ask, In what sense *know?* Does the writer mean historically,
or experientially, or mystically, or some other way? The frequency of the
use of the word "know" or "knowledge" insists on its importance and thus
compels us to probe its meaning. Two, to be Christian is to remember the
truth that has been imparted, but again, what particular truth? Is "truth"
a general term for the entire content of the faith, or is one feature of the
faith so central or so in danger of being lost that the repeated call to remember has that one line of the tradition in mind? So answer number two
raises question number two. And three, to be a Christian is to avoid being
seduced by the deceivers among you, but again, what deceivers? Do they
lay moral traps or is perversion of doctrine their game? Or both? And so
answer number three raises question number three. But at least these
three answers to our question of the text will serve well as magnets to draw
the filings of detail scattered through the letter into one more coherent
whole.

A WAY TO BEGIN

We have now moved around in this epistle sufficiently to offer a statement, preliminary but not uninformed, on each of the four questions with which one approaches any writing. All of us reserve the right, however, to change our view on any of these matters once our study together has been completed.

What Kind of Literature Is It?

Second Peter is a letter, one of the seven general letters of the New Testament. Granted, not all the features of a letter as we have come to know them in the Pauline correspondence (signature, address, greeting, thanksgiving or eulogy, message, closing greetings, farewell) are present here, but not all the elements must be present in order for a document to be a letter. It is clear that the writer intended 2 Peter to be received as such. The epistolary form had become so popular in the church that the use of the form may have in and of itself gained a more receptive audience for the message. Having said that, it is important to recall that a letter may contain other discernible forms, such as hymns, lists of household duties, vice and virtue lists, homilies, liturgies, etc., many of which we saw in 1 Peter. A closer look at 2 Peter reveals similarities to literary forms known from other sources. For example, one scholar has noted the apparent kinship between chapter 1 and an imperial decree. Such decrees identified the celebrating community, extolled the virtues and contributions of the community's benefactor, and finally, made recommendations for appropriate recognition of the benefactor. Although these features are not all highly visible in 2 Peter 1, such a reading is possible. More evident to the nonspecialist is the apologetic nature of chapter 3. An apology was not an "I'm sorry" but an argument in defense of a particular position. Apologies for the Christian faith became popular in Christian communities, the substance of the arguments being shaped very much by the addressees, whether emperors, philosophers, or leaders of other religions. Whether or not such persons ever read them, apologies gave instruction and encouragement to the believers. Second Peter 3 is or contains an apology for a particular view of the end of the world and divine judgment, addressed to Christians who are being influenced to abandon such a view.

Overall, however, 2 Peter has been increasingly identified as a letter in the mold of a valedictory or farewell address, sometimes called a testament. The farewell address is familiar to readers of the Bible: Jacob (Gen.

47:29–49:32), Moses (Deuteronomy 1—3, 28—31), Joshua (Joshua 23—24), and Samuel (1 Samuel 12) gave valedictory speeches, as did Jesus (John 14—16), Stephen (Acts 7) and Paul (Acts 20:18–35). A collection of such addresses can be found in the extracanonical (not included among the books of the Bible) writing, *Testament of the Twelve Patriarchs.* The pattern of this literary form is rather standard: The speaker is approaching death, on the horizon are problems for the followers left behind, but they are charged to be faithful in view of the retribution and reward of God. In the case of 2 Peter, the one dying is Simeon Peter and the approaching crisis consists of false and deceptive prophets. As we move through the letter, we will often refer to this pattern in the main body of the text.

Who Wrote the Letter?

The epistle carries the name of Simeon Peter, but as we discussed in introducing 1 Peter, that did not necessarily mean that Peter himself was the author. The name and influence of significant leaders were perpetuated by their circle of disciples. Writing in the name of a leader posed no ethical problem for the ancients, and especially in farewell addresses. For example, Deuteronomy is a sermon or series of sermons to Israel in King Josiah's time from the lips of Moses as a farewell speech. In other words, this is what Moses would say to us in our new situation.

What is the message of Peter to a church in a different time and place? We can be fairly confident that Simon Peter was dead when 2 Peter was written. The mount of transfiguration has now become "the holy mountain" (1:18); reverence having replaced reporting. The message "spoken through your apostles" (3:2) refers to the apostolic tradition that the writer's generation must not forget. And most persuasive of all the evidence is that according to 3:15–16, Paul's letters had already been collected and were regarded as scripture. Given the strong tradition that Peter died in Rome in the early 60s, we are certainly reading a letter from a Christian leader of a later generation who honors the name and the message of Simon Peter.

To Whom Was the Letter Written?

Given the absence of references to places or names (other than Peter), and given the widespread nature of the church conditions reflected in the letter, we can not, upon further reading, add to the description of the recipients given earlier. They are Gentile Christians, possibly in Asia Minor, who are coming under the influence of false teachers. They seem to be particularly vulnerable, given the extent to which their faith has apparently moved away from the apostolic tradition and mixed with current philosophies and lifestyles. They seem especially attracted to offers of freedom and of life free of trouble. The desire to be free of burdens may have prompted relieving themselves of the doctrine of the second coming and judgment. On that matter we will proceed more thoroughly when we explore chapter 3.

For What Purpose Was the Letter Written?

The answer is already implied in what has been said thus far. The apostolic era is now past, an era that the author assumes was free of schism and heresy but that carried prophecies of the coming of these evils on the church. Those prophecies are now coming true; false prophets and heretics plague the church. They are not outsiders; they are within the membership (2:13). At work is a double heresy, theological and ethical. The writer understands that the two are related; that is, corrupt living grows out of erroneous doctrine. The point is well taken. Those who glibly say that beliefs do not matter, only how one lives is important, miss the connection. Our lives differ because our beliefs and values are different. In the case of 2 Peter, the writer believes that abandoning the doctrine of the second coming by the heretics and those whom they deceive has eroded the moral and ethical life of the church. He believes a pillar has been pulled from the foundation of Christian living. The primary purpose of the letter is to warn the church, to counter the false prophets, and to rehabilitate the teaching concerning the coming day of the Lord. As we shall see, the lines of argument are several, but in essence the writer's message is a call to remember and to return to the apostolic tradition, authorized by the prophets, the word of Jesus, and the apostles. As mentioned earlier, the author is greatly exercised over the state of the church and in his fervor repeats himself often, heaps condemnation on the false teachers, slips into name calling, and warns everyone of the final judgment. But the letter itself is a testimony to hope; else why write at all? Many in the church prefer to listen to other preachers, but this one does have something to say, and it is he who is in the pulpit now.

OUTLINE OF SECOND PETER

Salutation   1:1–2
God's Blessings and Our Response   1:3–11
   What God Has Done   1:3–4
   What We Are to Do   1:5–11

Commentary

SALUTATION
2 Peter 1:1–2

> 1:1 **Simeon Peter, a servant and apostle of Jesus Christ.**
> **To those who have received a faith as precious as ours through the right-**
> **eousness of our God and Savior Jesus Christ:**
> ² **May grace and peace be yours in abundance in the knowledge of God**
> **and of Jesus our Lord.**

Reading a letter that begins with the writer's signature takes some getting used to, but it is refreshing in its difference, and makes sense. We turn to the signature before reading a letter anyway, and we expect from the signature not only the identity of the writer but hints about the letter's purpose and the relationship of writer and reader. The signature "Jenny" signals a message quite different from one signed "Dr. Jennifer." In the epistle before us, the signature stirs interest and curiosity, joining as it does the old Hebrew name Simeon and the new name Jesus gave this man, Peter (Matt. 16:18). Was this an attempt to join old and new in a letter that will champion so strongly the tradition from the prophets, Jesus, and the apostles? Perhaps. Or maybe it is a union of Hebrew and Greek in an effort to announce inclusivity at the outset. Again, perhaps.

But perhaps also we may be reading too much into the name. The writer's designation of himself as both servant (slave) and apostle is not so surprising as the apparent distance between the two words might imply. Peter was called by Jesus to be an apostle (Mark 3:13–19), but that did not mean he ceased to be a servant any more than being called to be a shepherd meant he was no longer a sheep following the great Shepherd (John 21:15–19). We have grown accustomed to this word combination in Paul (for example, Rom. 1:1) and recognize its modern counterpart in those good ministers who allow no ecclesiastical elevations to erase the mem-

95

ory of ordination. After all, it began with Jesus himself at whose baptism two prophecies were joined, Isaiah's suffering servant (Isa. 42:1) and the Psalmist's royal son (Psalm 2:7).

The address of the letter is as broad and inclusive as can be found in the church's correspondence: To all Christians everywhere. However, some phrases within the address are quite striking. To say the readers "have received a faith" (v. 1) may surprise those who think of faith as what we do in response to God's act, and so it is. However, to emphasize God's grace, the New Testament is not hesitant to speak of both faith and repentance as gifts of God (Acts 11:18; Rom. 12:3; 1 Cor. 12:9). That the readers' faith is "as precious as ours" ("share equally with us in the privileges of faith," REB) means that their distance in time and place from the apostles does not in any way make them secondhand Christians. As Jesus said to Thomas, "Have you believed because you have seen me? Blessed are those who have not seen and yet have come to believe" (John 20:29). And how so? Because we all received equally from a righteous God; that is, from a God who behaves toward us fairly and justly, in both judgment and mercy. Whether the writer intends us to hear "our God" and "Savior Jesus Christ" as separate or as one is unclear. To refer to Jesus Christ as *our God* and Savior would be unusual but not unique in the New Testament (see similar expressions in John 1:18; Rom. 9:5; Heb. 1:8). The Roman governor Pliny reported that Christians in Asia Minor sang hymns to Christ "as to a god." The writer here is oblivious to the big christological furor to come later, fed in part by the ambiguity of language such as this.

The greeting (v. 2) is in part familiar to us from 1 Peter 1:2 and kindred expressions in Pauline correspondence. The new element lies in the added phrase, "in the knowledge of God and of Jesus our Lord." This is not an unimportant addition inasmuch as knowledge of God and of Christ is of central importance to this letter (1:2, 3, 5, 6, 8; 2:20; 3:18). In fact, the writer opens and closes with knowledge as both possession and goal of Christians (1:2; 3:18). Perhaps we should pause here and acknowledge that some among us might be uncomfortable with 2 Peter on this matter. Those who have grown up in the broad currents of anti-intellectualism in this country may be suspicious of knowledge as the enemy of faith ("He had a strong faith until he went to the university"). And some uneasiness with knowledge is not without justification. Paul found the knowledgeable ones in the Corinthian church to be puffed up, arrogant, and impatient with the less enlightened (1 Corinthians 8). Widespread in early Christianity was the disturbing presence of persons we generally refer to as Gnostics (the ones who know) who claimed a special secret and saving knowledge of God, of the cosmos, and of all matters spiritual. Whether by birth, by revelation, or by mental effort, these boasted of knowing what only a few know: Who we are, whence we came, whither we go.

But every truth has its perversions, and the truth is, knowledge of God is desirable and good. It is the promise of the new covenant: "they shall all know me, from the least of them to the greatest" (Jer. 31:34). It is the purpose of Christ's coming (John 1:18) because to know God is life eternal (John 17:3). It is a work of the Holy Spirit to enable an understanding of the things of God (1 Cor. 2:9–10). The writer of 2 Peter, then, is at the healthy center of the Christian tradition when he speaks so positively of knowledge of God and of Christ. Such knowledge made it possible to escape the defilements of the world (2:20) and in this knowledge the faithful are to continue to grow (3:18). Such reminders are very important for a church besieged by false teachers who in their lack of knowledge, twist and pervert the scriptures for their own purpose (3:16). As Shakespeare put it, "There is no error so gross but some sober brow will bless it with a proper text."

GOD'S BLESSINGS AND OUR RESPONSE
2 Peter 1:3–11

Through the strong influence of Paul's letters, we have come to expect as the fourth element in an epistle (after signature, address, and greeting) a thanksgiving or a eulogy, that is, a word of blessing or praise to God (1 Peter 1:3; Eph. 1:3). The thanksgiving or eulogy is usually rather lengthy, opening with an expression of gratitude or praise and continuing with a presentation in brief of the principal themes of the letter. Thus the mood of the letter and the expectations of the readers are set. It might seem at first that 2 Peter 1:3–11 departs from the pattern, but in fact it does not. Beginning with a praiselike affirmation of God's power and goodness, this unit continues with a recital of the benefits of God's action toward believers, exhorts them to a moral seriousness that will secure them against the loss of those benefits, and anticipates entry into the eternal kingdom. Here, in germ, is not only the writer's message now to be unfolded but also a statement of the very core items of the faith apparently discarded by the false prophets, both in their persons and their preaching.

What God Has Done (2 Peter 1:3–4)

1:3 **His divine power has given us everything needed for life and godliness, through the knowledge of him who called us by his own glory and goodness.**
4 **Thus he has given us, through these things, his precious and very great**

promises, so that through them you may escape from the corruption that is in the world because of lust, and may become participants of the divine nature.

The language in these two verses is lofty and flourishing, as is appropriate in speaking of God and what God has done. Recall the grand excesses of hymns in which worshipers push the limits of ordinary speech to sing of God's power and goodness. Even so, the language here is without parallel in the New Testament.

What is being said? First, the readers are reminded that God has not called us out from our pasts and then left us to our own resources to remain faithful. We have been furnished, equipped, empowered for a full life, marked with the quality of God's own holiness. That culture, not unlike our own, spoke of self-discovery and self-fulfillment, and perhaps our author would not have balked at such language as long as the acknowledgment of God's initiative was preserved: "His divine power his given us . . . who called us. . . . thus he has given us."

Second, this new life is effected through knowledge of God through Jesus Christ (see the discussion of "knowledge" at v. 2). Since this knowledge transforms, it is not only mental but emotional, spiritual, and volitional as well. Having said this, let us avoid allowing knowledge of God to become too broad and vague. The author will insist that saving knowledge of God is joined to the tradition in which the readers have been thoroughly instructed (1:12–15).

And finally, this life in God is not only present but has always before it the promise of moving from this corrupt and transient world into the realm where we shall be incorruptible and immortal as God is. The terminology here is from the culture of the writer and readers. Many philosophies and religions of the Hellenistic world spoke of, longed for, and held up the promise of taking on the divine nature; that is, immortality. But notice here the Christian modifications. The corruption of the world is not by reason of its creation but "because of lust" (v. 4). In other words, the conversion from this life to the next is not achieved simply by dying and therefore passing from mortality to immortality. Rather the change is moral and ethical. It is the knowledge of God as revealed in Jesus Christ and not simply a funeral which provides "entry into the eternal kingdom" (v. 11). That possessing the divine nature includes holiness as well as immortality is also a Christian correction of a popular notion in that culture. With such modifications, the affirmation of 1:4 is not really so distant from other New Testament expressions of the promise. For example,

"Beloved, we are God's children now; what we will be has not yet been revealed. What we do know is this: when he is revealed, we will be like him, for we will see him as he is" (1 John 3:2). Or again, "What is sown is perishable, what is raised is imperishable. It is sown in dishonor, it is raised in glory. It is sown in weakness, it is raised in power. It is sown a physical body, it is raised a spiritual body" (1 Cor. 15:42–44a). Ancient theology expressed this belief in a single line: "He became as we are, so that we might become as he is."

What We Are to Do (2 Peter 1:5–11)

1:5 **For this very reason, you must make every effort to support your faith with goodness, and goodness with knowledge, 6 and knowledge with self-control, and self-control with endurance, and endurance with godliness, 7 and godliness with mutual affection, and mutual affection with love. 8 For if these things are yours and are increasing among you, they keep you from being ineffective and unfruitful in the knowledge of our Lord Jesus Christ. 9 For anyone who lacks these things is nearsighted and blind, and is forgetful of the cleansing of past sins. 10 Therefore, brothers and sisters, be all the more eager to confirm your call and election, for if you do this, you will never stumble. 11 For in this way, entry into the eternal kingdom of our Lord and Savior Jesus Christ will be richly provided for you.**

Attention now turns to the ways in which the beneficiaries of God's power and goodness respond. This movement of thought is familiar from both testaments. At Sinai, Israel first heard, " I am the LORD your God, who brought you out of the land of Egypt, out of the house of slavery" (Exod. 20:2), and then the moral and ethical instructions for God's people (Exod. 20:1–17). In the Sermon on the Mount, Jesus first pronounced God's blessings and then outlined how God's people are to live together (Matt. 5:1–7:29). God's grace and human responsibility belong together. The former without the latter is cheapened, degenerating into empty spirituality and the subjective captivity of the gospel; the latter without the former elevates itself into works-righteousness with attendant pride or despair. The writer here is not worried that God's grace will make his readers passive or that their efforts will create a merit system of salvation. They are to "make every effort" (v. 5); they are to grow in the Christian graces (v. 8); they are to be careful not to stumble (v. 10). But any such achievement will but confirm their call and election (v. 10); that is, what God has already done for them. All this is to say that sound Christian theology issues in sound Christian living which is effective and fruitful (v. 8). Knowledge of God is not simply a discussion topic over afternoon tea; rather it is character changing and society changing. Passive belief is nearsighted in viewing the world and blind and forgetful in viewing the self (v. 9). One's baptism is to be lived out in continual renewal. Our forebears in the faith understood this and issued to the membership of the church a sober warning by listing among the seven deadly sins *akedia*, sloth; in other words, "I don't care anymore." Our writer is hardly less vivid: "For it would have been better for them never to have known the way of righteousness than, after knowing it, to turn back from the holy commandment that was passed on to them" (2:21).

The theme, then, of 2 Peter 1:5–11 is Christian conduct, and the presentation of this theme is dominated by the catalog of virtues in verses 5–7. The entire unit is framed by the word translated "support" in verse 5 (the REB translates it "add") and "provided" in verse 11. The same word appears as "supplies" in 2 Cor. 9:10. The message seems to be: If you make provision for your faith with the following virtues (v. 5), God will make provision for your entry into the eternal kingdom (v. 11). The word translated "support" or "provide" is an interesting one. Its noun form is the Greek word "chorus" and in its verb form meant "to direct a chorus." If the writer had this original meaning in mind, then in verse 5 he is saying "direct the chorus of your Christian life" or "orchestrate your Christian life" in the following way. The word came to mean, especially in Athens, "to support, to equip, or to make provision for the chorus." Most translators prefer, and perhaps wisely so, this second meaning.

Lists of virtues as well as lists of vices were fairly common among Greek philosophers and moralists prior to and including the early Christian era. They are found in the wisdom literature and more philosophical writings of later Judaism and soon became popular in Christian circles. The reason lies in the list itself: These are qualities to be welcomed in both synagogue and church. In spite of all the warnings against the embrace of secular culture, many Christian leaders were pleased to find among Greek and Roman writers the extolling of qualities in the good life with which Moses and Jesus would agree. Some Christian writers argued that the appearance of these virtue lists among non-Christians was proof that God was also at work among "the heathen."

The shape of the list in 1:5–7 was probably the work of orators who often gave to material forms that afforded ease of memory both for the speaker and the listener. Notice the rhythm of repetition and addition:

> Faith with goodness,
> goodness with knowledge,
> knowledge with self-control,
> self-control with endurance,
> endurance with godliness,
> godliness with mutual affection,
> mutual affection with love.

This is not to say that the writer simply accepted a list found in the culture. On the contrary, it seems evident that, under the influence of the gospel, changes were made in some words in the list and the order in which they occur. Outside Christian circles, knowledge occurred frequently on virtue lists, sometimes first, sometimes last, both positions indicating importance. When faith was listed, it was not in the sense of trust in a god but rather as faithfulness or loyalty. Self-control appeared on many lists, and Paul as well as 2 Peter embraced it as a Christian quality (Gal. 5:22–23). In recent times self-control has, in some quarters, lost favor due to the more favorable attention given to self-expression and release from inhibitions. Endurance, in a general sense meaning "patience," came to refer among Christians to that quality of holding up under persecution and being able to wait for the Lord's coming. Goodness or virtue, that is, right conduct based on self-discipline, may have been taken unaltered from the Greeks. It took on new importance later when the church developed programs of vows and disciplines of the soul. Godliness or piety is more common on Greek than on Christian lists. Among the Greeks it referred to being genuinely religious, living in deference to the gods. Christians baptized the word (1 Tim. 6:11; 2 Peter 1:3) to give it the particular sense of emulating in one's life qualities of God as revealed in Jesus Christ.

Two features of the list invite special comment. First, distinction is made between mutual affection and love. Mutual affection is literally "love of one's brothers and sisters" (*philadelphia*) and is an essential component of church life. But that is just the point: mutual affection, reciprocal love, pertains to life in the church, to the fellowship. Beyond that, however, is love, *agape*. Love does not require reciprocity; it includes the stranger, and even the enemy. It behaves favorably and helpfully toward the other regardless of who the other is or what the other has done. God is love, and God is kind even to the ungrateful and selfish (Luke 6:35).

Second, it is not accidental that the list begins with faith and ends with love. This faith/love combination was for Paul a favorite summation of the

Christian life (Gal. 5:6), and beyond Paul the church found in these two words the heart of the matter. Bishop Ignatius, writing to the church in Ephesus early in the second century, expressed it this way: "The beginning is faith and the end is love, and when the two are joined in unity, it is God" (*To the Ephesians* 14:1).

THE FAREWELL ADDRESS: AN OPENING PERSONAL WORD
2 Peter 1:12–15

1:12 **Therefore I intend to keep on reminding you of these things, though you know them already and are established in the truth that has come to you.** [13] **I think it right, as long as I am in this body, to refresh your memory,** [14] **since I know that my death will come soon, as indeed our Lord Jesus Christ has made clear to me.** [15] **And I will make every effort so that after my departure you may be able at any time to recall these things.**

As stated in the introduction, this commentary is structured on the view that 2 Peter is a testament; that is, a valedictory or farewell address. Granted, it is offered to the churches as a letter and as a letter it desired to be received; 1:1–11 and 3:17–18 make that clear. But the body of the document, 1:12–3:16, bears all the marks of a farewell address. And what does that mean? In form, it means that the text will have at least three features:

1. There will be a statement to the effect that the one in whose name the message is presented is approaching death.
2. The history or tradition shared by the speaker and listeners is either recited in summary or referred to frequently as the prized possession of the group, never to be relinquished.
3. Dire warnings about dangers within and without underscore the call to faithfulness.

In function, a valedictory marks the end of an era; the death of Moses or of Joshua, the death of Jesus or of a major apostle. In the letter before us, the apostolic era is past and we are dealing with what New Testament scholar Raymond Brown refers to as "the churches the apostles left behind." It is a critical time. Tradition has replaced the living voice, and the legacy of the past must be preserved. This urgent need put pressure on the church to choose its leadership carefully, to teach its membership thoroughly, and to define "the true faith" precisely. An era devoted heavily to retrenching and defending the faith was not the exciting time that the past had been, but without it would there have been a future? Hence the writer says, "I intend to keep on reminding you of these things. . . . I think it is right, as long as I am in this body, to refresh your memory. . . . And I will make every effort so that after my departure you may be able at any time to recall these things" (1:12–13, 15).

Of course, what sets the tone of the valedictory is the announcement of approaching death. Final words are very important, carefully chosen, not to be forgotten. When the church gathers around the bed of a dying leader, it leans forward, careful not to miss a word. Verse 14, then, is intended to affect everything that is said in the remainder of the letter: "I know that my death will come soon, as indeed our Lord Jesus Christ has made clear to me." This statement is obviously a reference to the epilogue to the Gospel of John in which Jesus indicates to Simon Peter the martyr's death that awaits him (John 21:18–19). The tradition is strong that Peter's death did occur in Rome during the reign of Nero in the sixth decade of the Christian era.

The brevity of the announcement of approaching death should not cause the reader to lose sight of its importance for both the mood and the message of the letter. Perhaps we should pause before proceeding and let Simon Peter's words join those of other great leaders whose valedictories are preserved in Scripture.

Listen to Moses: "I am now one hundred twenty years old. I am no longer able to get about, and the LORD has told me, 'You shall not cross over this Jordan' " (Deut. 31:2).

And to Joshua: "I am now old and well advanced in years. . . . I am about to go the way of all the earth" (Josh. 23:2, 14).

And to Paul: "And now I know that none of you, among whom I have gone about proclaiming the kingdom, will ever see my face again" (Acts 20:25).

And, of course, to Jesus: "A little while, and you will no longer see me, and again a little while, and you will see me. . . . After Jesus had spoken these words, he looked up to heaven and said, 'Father, the hour has come' " (John 16:16; 17:1).

THE FAREWELL ADDRESS: THE MESSAGE STATED AND CONFIRMED
2 Peter 1:16–21

Following the autobiographical note, the substance of the address unfolds as follows: the statement of the issue and the beginning of the defense of the apostolic tradition; indictment of the opponents on both doctrinal and ethical grounds; the continuation of the defense of the apostolic tradition.

The Statement (2 Peter 1:16a)

1:16a **For we did not follow cleverly devised myths when we made known to you the power and coming of our Lord Jesus Christ.**

The issue being debated by the writer and certain teachers in the church is simply stated: "the power and coming of our Lord Jesus Christ." The phrase itself could refer to the first coming ("coming" or "arrival" translates the Greek word *parousia*) of Christ, the event we celebrate at Advent. Christ's coming in Bethlehem was not without power and glory: angelic messengers, heavenly hosts, an unusual star, a king shaking on his throne, and wealthy magi from a distant land. That event, too, was eschatological; that is, it marked the end of one world and the beginning of another. But in the present context "the power and coming" refers to the second coming, the return of Christ in the final enthronement of God's Son over all forces to the contrary. This understanding of the *parousia* is present not only in this letter (3:4, 12) but rather widely in the New Testament (see for example, Matt. 24:3; 1 Cor. 15:23; James 5:7–8).

The teaching about the second coming may be for some Christians today a matter of less than primary importance. While some have been preoccupied with this doctrine, often being so bold as to predict time and place, others have reacted in embarrassed silence. But for 2 Peter, the issue is important for at least two reasons. First, it is firmly imbedded in the apostolic tradition and to deny it is to raise serious questions about the legacy of saving truth of which the writer is a strong proponent. Obviously, the author is not an advocate of the church's continual reassessment and reinterpretation of the positions held by a previous generation. The apostolic tradition is for him a package of truth to be handed on, although only this one component of that tradition is under discussion here, the remainder of its content lying outside our view.

The other reason the second coming is important for 2 Peter is that for the author (and many others) this teaching is foundational for the moral and ethical life of Christians. The letter will argue vigorously that to pull away from the conviction of the Lord's return is to release in the church all kinds of permissive and irresponsible behavior. Church history demonstrates that wherever Christian conduct has been predicated on the fear and anticipation generated by this doctrine, the loss of that belief has had moral and ethical fallout. Likewise, wherever the Christian life has been prompted and nourished by other understandings of one's relation to Christ, the delay of the *parousia* or the slackened interest in this teaching has not been erosive of Christian behavior and relationships.

As for "the power and coming of our Lord Jesus Christ" in the text before us, two observations can be made. First, the readers have already been taught on this matter. It is not a doctrine new to them nor does it need to be reviewed at length. The writer is but refreshing their memory concerning what "we made known to you" (v. 16). Second, some opponents of the doctrine have classified it as a myth, a speculation, a dramatic story created by Jesus' followers, perhaps to help control the behavior of subsequent generations of believers. The writer will in turn charge these opponents with disseminating deceptive myths and speculations (2:1–3). The truth versus the myth is a form of debate rather common among both Jewish and Christian writers (see, for example, 1 Tim. 1:4; 4:7; 6:20; 2 Tim. 2:16; Titus 1:14). To make his claim to the truth hold up, the author moves immediately to support his statement.

Its Confirmation (2 Peter 1:16b–21)

1:16b **but we had been eyewitnesses of his majesty.** [17] **For he received honor and glory from God the Father when that voice was conveyed to him by the Majestic Glory, saying, "This is my Son, my Beloved, with whom I am well pleased."** [18] **We ourselves heard this voice come from heaven, while we were with him on the holy mountain.**

[19] **So we have the prophetic message more fully confirmed. You will do well to be attentive to this as to a lamp shining in a dark place, until the day dawns and the morning star rises in your hearts.** [20] **First of all you must understand this, that no prophecy of scripture is a matter of one's own interpretation,** [21] **because no prophecy ever came by human will, but men and women moved by the Holy Spirit spoke from God.**

Although he will add to the argument later, the writer at this early point develops a threefold defense of the apostolic teaching that Christ will come in power and glory. This truth, he says, has triple confirmation: eyewitnesses, the Hebrew prophets, and the Holy Spirit.

As for being eyewitnesses, Peter is bold in his assertion: "we had been eyewitnesses" (v. 16); "we ourselves heard this voice come from heaven" (v. 18); "we were with him on the holy mountain(v. 18)." But how can he argue that he and other apostles have personally witnessed the *parousia* when it is an event of the future? In a most intriguing line of thought, the writer appeals to the Synoptic accounts of the Transfiguration (Matt. 17:1–13; Mark 9:2–13; Luke 9:28–36) with which he assumes his readers are familiar. However, the readers are given an interpretation of the Transfiguration unlike that provided by the Gospel contexts. For example, in the Gospels Jesus has for the first time introduced the subject of his own death. Immediately, the readers and Peter, James, and John are given this extraordinary vision of who Jesus really is, the glorious Son of God. In Luke, the transfigured Jesus is discussing his approaching death with Moses and Elijah. Hence another interpretation of the Transfiguration is that it placed Jesus in the larger picture of God's salvation history. Or in Mark 9:1, the prophecy that some of those present would not die before seeing the kingdom come with power is followed immediately by the story of the Transfiguration. Apparently the prophecy is thus fulfilled. Perhaps the Gospels afford other meanings of the Transfiguration, relating it to the resurrection or to the ascension. Here, however, it is offered as confirmation of the second coming. How so?

Perhaps the thinking is like this: The Christ of the second coming will be enthroned as God's Son and appropriately described as possessing majesty, glory, and power. But how can one attribute these qualities to the crucified Nazarene? We have seen his majesty and glory, says Peter; we have heard God's voice declare, "This is my Son." If it has happened, it can happen, and it will happen. The Transfiguration is not only a prophecy of the second coming but a clear demonstration of it.

And speaking of prophecy, says the writer, this teaching is firmly grounded in the Old Testament (1:19). No particular citation is given, but this is not unusual. In Luke 24 there are repeated references to all that is in the Old Testament concerning Christ (vv. 25, 27, 44–47), but the reader is given no clue as to what those citations are. In 2 Peter 1:19–21 the writer may be assuming that from their prior instruction the readers know to which prophecy he refers. We are the ones who do not know. Shall we make a guess? In the prophecies of Balaam, to be discussed in chapter 2, appears the line "a star shall come out of Jacob" (Num. 24:17). The use of "morning star" in verse 19 makes Numbers 24 a candidate for "the prophetic message more fully confirmed." And since the subject is the coming of Christ, Dan. 7:13–14, much used in New Testament passages about the coming of the son of Man, must be considered. However, my own guess—and that is all it is—is Psalm 2. The reason? The word confirmed in prophecy is that which was stated in verses 17–18, the Transfiguration story. There reference is made to the holy mountain (Psalm 2:6) and the voice from heaven quotes Psalm 2:7:

"I have set my king on Zion, my holy hill."

I will tell of the decree of the LORD:
He said to me, "You are my son;
    today I have begotten you."

But regardless of the text or texts the writer and readers have in mind, three important statements about biblical prophecy are made. First, they function as a lamp in a dark place. Prophecy gives to the faith community direction, focus, and hope in this dark world. However, when the day dawns, when Christ shall appear, prophecy will no longer be needed. As Paul says, "as for prophecies, they will come to an end" (1 Cor. 13:8). When that age dawns, Christ the morning star will appear. Strikingly, this word translated "morning star" appears nowhere else in either testament although a similar expression occurs in Rev. 22:16, translated "the bright morning star." That the word used here appears often in non-Christian Greek literature makes it appropriate to remind ourselves that Christians of every age use the vocabulary of their cultures to speak to those cultures about the faith. And that the morning star will rise "in your hearts" reminds us that the day of the Lord will not only be cosmic in its immensity but also personally transforming in its effect.

Second, the writer says that scriptural prophecy is not properly handled by private interpreters (v. 20). Undoubtedly, this word is aimed at the opponents who take the very same scriptures that the author understands as confirming the apostolic teaching about the Lord's coming and give them a contrary interpretation. If these false teachers twist the meaning of difficult passages in Paul, "as they do the other scriptures" (3:16), then we may safely assume they did the same with the prophecies of the Old Testament. But does not every Christian have the right to his or her own interpretation of scripture? Is not one interpretation as good as another? If not, then who decides? In response, 2 Peter enunciates two principles that were long observed in the Christian community. First, interpretation of scripture is not a private or individual exercise; rather it is a function of the community. Of course, the church has always had its teachers and scholars who preserve, translate, and interpret scripture, but they do not function in isolation from the faith community. The Bible is the church's book and finally all interpreters bring their understandings back to the church. Some measure of isolation is needed, of course, for scholars and teachers to do their research, but acknowledged or not, they work within the larger circle of the community that looks to the scripture for meaning, encouragement, and correction.

I recall years ago hearing a preacher use an Old Testament text prohibiting a person born out of wedlock from serving at the temple altar to argue that illegitimate children could not enter God's presence; that is, they could not go to heaven. Within an hour of that sermon the minister was dismissed by the congregation. As a visitor I agreed with the church's position against such preaching, but I was curious to know the theological or scriptural ground for decision. My query was answered by the lay leader, by no means a biblical scholar: "We would never do that to those children, and we believe that surely God is as Christian as we are, so that preacher was wrong in his use of that scripture." Not bad.

If the church in the time of 2 Peter had no pew Bibles nor owned individual copies of sacred texts and yet suffered the schisms created by private interpretations, just think how much greater this problem became with the advent of the printing press. Do not misunderstand; the availability of scripture to every family and person was and is a blessing beyond measuring. However, when I can sit alone with my Bible on my lap, I can easily be seduced into becoming my own church, and I might even cease to join the assembly that provided the scripture and that continually seeks to hear aright the Word of God.

The second principle of interpretation offered by 2 Peter is kin to the first: The apostolic tradition is a proper guide for arriving at the meaning of the text. This principle was operative in the determination of whether a particular Christian writing was to be included in the New Testament, and it was operative in interpreting those writings that were included. The assumptions are that the apostles preserved the revelation from God in the person, work, and words of Jesus, and that it is appropriate to measure the claims of any prophet, evangelist, or teacher by that apostolic tradition. Spoken and unspoken, sometimes quietly and sometimes heatedly, that principle is still operative to this day.

Having said that prophecy is in effect until the dawn of the new age and that prophecy is not to be privately interpreted, 2 Peter 1:19–21 makes a third and final statement about biblical prophecy: Prophecies in scripture are not of human origin but came by the prompting of the Holy Spirit (Acts 28:25; 2 Tim. 3:16). Unlike false prophets who spoke easily and convincingly the message people wanted to hear, God's prophets were often reluctant and resistant, knowing God's word is sometimes painful and unwelcomed. But God's Spirit pushed them beyond their natural reticence to speak the truth appropriate to the occasion. The corollary of this understanding is that the interpreter of those prophecies possesses that same Spirit of God. The author is making this claim for himself and for the apostolic tradition: The teaching about the coming of the Lord is both given and received by means of the Holy Spirit.

This word about the Holy Spirit brings to a conclusion the writer's threefold confirmation of the message concerning "the power and coming of our Lord Jesus Christ" (v. 16): We were eyewitnesses; the message is according to prophecy; the Holy Spirit both gave this message and enables the church to receive it.

THE FAREWELL ADDRESS: ATTACK UPON
THE OPPONENTS
2 Peter 2:1–22

A common feature of biblical valedictories is the prediction of the future for the faithful left behind following the death of the leader. This prophecy of what is to come is in reality a literary device for describing what is in fact the present circumstance of the readers. In other words, the dying leader spells out what is to come and the readers say, "It is true; that is exactly what is happening here now." And the prophecy is filled with dire warnings; the way ahead is fraught with dangers and for the people of God the future is a mine field. The problems may lie within the weak faith of the people themselves. So said the dying Moses: "I know that after my death you will surely act corruptly, turning aside from the way that I have commanded you. In time to come trouble will befall you, because you will do what is evil in the sight of the LORD" (Deut. 31:29). Or the difficulties may come as outside opposition to the believers. So warned Jesus in his farewell to the disciples: "They will put you out of the synagogues. Indeed, an hour is coming when those who kill you will think that by doing so they are offering worship to God. . . . I did not say these things to you from the beginning, because I was with you. But now I am going to him who sent me" (John 16:2, 4–5). And sometimes the crises to be faced are created by false teachers within the ranks of the faithful. Listen to Paul in two of his farewell addresses:

> I know that after I have gone, savage wolves will come in among you, not sparing the flock. Some even from your own group will come distorting the truth in order to entice the disciples to follow them. (Acts 20:29–30)
> For the time is coming when people will not put up with sound doctrine, but having itching ears, they will accumulate for themselves

teachers to suit their own desires, and will turn away from listening to the truth and wander away to myths. (2 Tim. 4:3–4)

It is in this last form that problems face the church of 2 Peter.

Portrait of the Opponents (2 Peter 2:1–3)

2:1 But false prophets also arose among the people, just as there will be false teachers among you, who will secretly bring in destructive opinions. They will even deny the Master who bought them—bringing swift destruction on themselves. 2 Even so, many will follow their licentious ways, and because of these teachers the way of truth will be maligned. 3 And in their greed they will exploit you with deceptive words. Their condemnation, pronounced against them along ago, has not been idle, and their destruction is not asleep.

Continuing the subject of prophecy (1:19–21), the writer acknowledges that the history of true prophecy is tainted by the appearance of false prophets. Sometimes these prophets openly opposed the word from God, but often they were seductive, insinuating, and deceptive. As in Israel, (see, for example, Jer. 5:12; 6:14; Ezek. 13:10), so also in the church. And chapters 2—3 make it abundantly clear that "there *will* be false teachers among you" (2:1) is to be understood as "there *are now* false teachers among you." But are we dealing with a phenomenon peculiar to the church addressed by 2 Peter? In other words, are the heretics here described peculiar to this particular congregation or group of congregations? We will have occasion when discussing Jude to note the clear literary connections between portions of Jude and 2 Peter 2. We will not at this point enter into questions of who is borrowing from whom and why there are modifications in remarkably similar material. However, it might be appropriate in the present discussion to ask what it might mean for a common body of material to be addressed to different readers by different writers. Are we dealing with a rather standardized and general attack on heretics in the church, whatever may be the particular contours of heresy in a specific situation? If so, then chapter 2 may not be as helpful as we would wish as a resource for reconstructing the life of the faith community being addressed. Fortunately for us, however, chapter 3 will return to the specific issue being debated, the second coming of Christ. Then we will be able, however generalized chapter 2 may seem, to resume the discussion opened at 1:16 and get a clearer picture of the particular turmoil among believers addressed in this letter.

The writer, of course, has his own agenda and point of view, but even so, distance from the congregation(s) addressed affords a kind of clarity that licenses the act of pointing out to the readers what they themselves may be too close to see. A foot soldier in the Civil War could provide us a record irreplaceable in its detail and authorized by firsthand experience. However, someone more removed from the fighting might be better able to help us understand the war. Likewise, the author, not being present (we remind ourselves that we do not know either the address or the return address of this letter) may help those present to recognize the false teachers among them.

How, then, are they characterized? They move among the people secretly. They deny the Master who bought them, and, like Balaam of old (see below), they sell their services for what they think is a higher bid. Such is the blindness of greed, which is for them a primary motive. To say they deny God or Christ is not to say that they have become atheists in a theological sense. Rather it is to say they are practical atheists; that is, persons who live as though there were no God. "Fools say in their hearts, 'There is no God.' They are corrupt, they do abominable deeds" (Psalm 14:1; see also Pss. 10:11, 13; 73:11). That these heretics are licentious (lecherous) may be the result of denying Christ, or the cause of it. Theology and lifestyle are a package; their errors are both doctrinal and moral. They dishonor the truth and use deceptive speech to ensnare and exploit.

And strikingly, the word "destructive" appears three times in this brief sketch of the opponents: their opinions are destructive; their activity is self-destructive; and God's destruction awaits them. The writer is fully aware that practical atheists have since ancient times apparently fared well without that reversal of fortune that could be understood as the judgment of God. They sometimes joked openly that God was asleep, or forgetful, or ignorant of what was going on (1 Kings 18:27; Psalms 10:11, 13; 73:11). In fact, some of the faithful saints, enduring social and economic hardships, acknowledged envy of the prospering wicked (Psalm 73:1–3). The truth is, says the writer, God is not slack in administering justice, as the heretics should have learned from biblical history. To a brief recital of God's former acts of judgment we are now treated.

God's Judgment (2 Peter 2:4–10)

> 2:4 **For if God did not spare the angels when they sinned, but cast them into hell and committed them to chains of deepest darkness to be kept until the judgment;** 5 **and if he did not spare the ancient world, even though he saved**

Noah, a herald of righteousness, with seven others, when he brought a flood on a world of the ungodly; 6 and if by turning the cities of Sodom and Gomorrah to ashes he condemned them to extinction and made them an example of what is coming to the ungodly; 7 and if he rescued Lot, a righteous man greatly distressed by the licentiousness of the lawless 8 (for that righteous man, living among them day after day, was tormented to his righteous soul by their lawless deeds that he saw and heard), 9 then the Lord knows how to rescue the godly from trial, and to keep the unrighteous under punishment until the day of judgment 10—especially those who indulge their flesh in depraved lust, and who despise authority.

Bold and willful, they are not afraid to slander the glorious ones.

The judgment of God involves both the punishment of the ungodly and the salvation of the faithful. But is there any evidence that God does, in fact, so act? The writer provides an answer in the form of a long sentence (vv. 4–10), beginning with the conditional "if" and concluding with "then." If this and this and this and this happened, then you have your answer; God certainly does know how to punish and to rescue. Three cases of punishment are offered: First, the sinning angels (sons of God) of Gen. 6:1–4. The author here reveals familiarity with a Jewish writing, *1 Enoch* (probably dated between the third century B.C. and the first century A.D.) which offers an elaborate interpretation of biblical history. According to *1 Enoch* 10, the angels of Genesis 6 became involved with earthly women and their offspring loosed war, violence, and idolatry in the world. As punishment, these angels were cast down into hell (*tartarus*) to be confined in dark pits until the final day of judgment. It is interesting that the writer assumes the readers not only knew *1 Enoch* but also regarded it as an authoritative account of God's activity.

The second example of divine judgment is the flood in the days of Noah (Genesis 6—8). Again, those punished are the ungodly. Because these warnings are for false teachers, one might expect examples of those who erred in doctrine or belief, but we have already seen, and will again in 2:12–22, that the writer joins doctrinal and moral failures as though related as cause and effect or perhaps as though each flowed from the other. And the final case of divine punishment is the destruction of the cities of Sodom and Gomorrah (Gen. 19:24).

But, as stated above, God's judgment involves also the rescue of the righteous. That God is able to save the faithful is established by the two classic cases, Noah and his family from the flood and Lot from the burning cities. And just in case the appropriateness of the recital is lost on those addressed by the letter, the point is driven home: This message is for those who indulge the flesh and despise the authority of the apostles who have given the truth that the heretics now mock (v. 10a).

The Opponents' Behavior Exposed (2 Peter 2:11–19)

2:11 . . . whereas angels, though greater in might and power, do not bring against them a slanderous judgment from the Lord. [12] These people, however, are like irrational animals, mere creatures of instinct, born to be caught and killed. They slander what they do not understand, and when those creatures are destroyed, they also will be destroyed, [13] suffering the penalty for doing wrong. They count it a pleasure to revel in the daytime. They are blots and blemishes, reveling in their dissipation while they feast with you. [14] They have eyes full of adultery, insatiable for sin. They entice unsteady souls. They have hearts trained in greed. Accursed children! [15] They have left the straight road and have gone astray, following the road of Balaam son of Bosor, who loved the wages of doing wrong, [16] but was rebuked for his own transgression; a speechless donkey spoke with a human voice and restrained the prophet's madness.

[17] These are waterless springs and mists driven by a storm; for them the deepest darkness has been reserved. [18] For they speak bombastic nonsense, and with licentious desires of the flesh they entice people who have just escaped from those who live in error. [19] They promise them freedom, but they themselves are slaves of corruption; for people are slaves to whatever masters them.

The letter turns at this point as though the writer could hear the adversaries saying, "We are familiar with those old stories of destruction, but what have they to do with us?" Or it is as though the preacher looked out at the congregation and saw those most in need of the message yawning on the back pew. In response the author goes on a rampage of rhetoric. Two words about the rhetoric: First, the writer continues to speak of the false teachers with the pronoun "they" as though these persons are not present and thus will not hear the reading of the letter. But they *are* present (v. 13). Otherwise, this whole section would be gossip about the absent, not a pronouncement to the present. Why, then, the "they"? One reason is that it enables the writer to sustain the farewell address form that predicts what will take place. In the future, "they" will do this or that. The use of "you" or "some of you" would have broken the valedictory pattern of the letter; that is, removing its predictive quality and making it a direct exhortation. In addition, the use of the third person "they" is also a tried and effective style of indictment. When the more confrontive "you" could close off listening and become counterproductive, a writer or speaker might speak indirectly as though describing persons not present. The audience, no longer defensive, listens, wondering to whom the message refers. It soon becomes apparent that the words are winged for them, but now it is too late; the message is heard. I listened recently to a strong sermon on an incendiary topic in which the preacher used the refrain, "We all know there are persons who. . . ." This method is not unlike Jesus' use of parables, following which some in the audience perceived he was talking to them.

The second word about the rhetoric has to do with its sharp denunciatory quality. These verses are admittedly distasteful to some of us, especially those drilled since childhood in the old maxim, "If you cannot say anything good about someone, then say nothing at all." The writer certainly finds no redeeming feature in the adversaries. In fact, an early reading of verses 10b–19 conjured up images from the evening news reports of rallies and counter-rallies over civil rights at which violent speech and ugly posters obscured the issues. Perhaps our ears will be helped if we understand that such speaking as we have here was a form of rhetoric (the art of persuasion) familiar to audiences of the time. Within the arsenal of the orators of the day was a rather standardized pattern called "in praise or in blame" of another person. Whether the flight of speech praised or blamed the other depended, of course, on the purpose of the address as did also the height of praise or the intensity of attack. Most likely the original readers were more able than subsequent ones to hear this section with understanding and without offense. In fact, they may have found in it a measure of sober entertainment—assuming they were not the ones denounced.

This section begins with a charge against the opponents most difficult for us to understand. In comments above on v. 10a, "despise authority" was interpreted as despising the authority or leadership of the apostles. That understanding seemed preferable to the view that the authority despised was civil; that is, governors or magistrates. Unlike 1 Peter, this letter does not portray a church dealing with a hostile society. Likewise, taking "authority" to refer to angelic beings in a celestial hierarchy (as in Eph. 1:21; Col. 1:16) whom the opponents despised seemed less appropriate to the context. However, at v. 10b the text clearly speaks of the heretics' abuse of angelic beings; they "slander [blaspheme] the glorious ones" ("celestial beings," REB). Why? What does that mean?

In Jude 8 this expression is used and is expanded by referring to an account of the death of Moses found in a late Jewish writing called *The As-*

sumption of Moses. The archangel Michael and the devil are arguing over the body of Moses, and the devil claims the right to Moses' body because, he said, Moses was a murderer, having killed an Egyptian. Michael refrained from charging the devil with blasphemy, leaving the judgment to God. Second Peter, apparently not wanting to get into the Michael versus Satan story, simply extracts from the account a general charge against the heretics. The charge runs something like this: Even an archangel does not presume to judge another angel (Satan was a rebellious angel), but these false teachers are so arrogant and audacious as to blaspheme angels. In a culture in which it was believed that good angels were executing God's will for the world and rebellious angels were trying to thwart God's purpose, to blaspheme angels was to shake the fist at heaven, to deny the existence of a spiritual order, and to announce one's triumphant secularity. Such a prideful sin was even more serious than despising the authority of the apostles.

(Note: References to *1 Enoch* and *The Assumption of Moses* may stir in the reader a curiosity about the intertestamental literature to which these two works belong, usually referred to as Pseudepigrapha. Collections of these writings, and in good English translation, were made available early in the century by R. H. Charles [*The Apocrypha and Pseudepigrapha of the Old Testament in English;* Oxford, 1913] and more recently by James Charlesworth [*The Old Testament Pseudepigrapha;* Doubleday, 1982].)

How, then, shall we summarize the description that follows? These heretics behave like animals. No, in offering their "religious services" for money, regardless of its source, they are inferior to Balaam's jackass, which spoke out against such greed in the ministry (see this remarkable story in Numbers 22). Without shame, they begin their revelries before dark and make a drinking party out of the church's fellowship meals and eucharistic gatherings. And it is not enough that their own lives are captive to greed and indulgence; they delight in luring into their circle unsteady novices in the faith, only yesterday in paganism and now out of the frying pan into the fire. And how are they able to entice these tender young souls? By promising them freedom, freedom from authority, from the moral demands of the Christian tradition, and from oppressive teachings such as the second coming of Christ. But the misled soon discover that the magnificent promise of freedom is fulfilled in a new kind of bondage.

This portrait of the adversaries is so much a contradiction of the values and relationships of the life we know as Christian that one wonders if the writer has not exaggerated their faults. No doubt there is some rhetorical flourish in the passage, but two factors need to be kept in mind. First, the Christian life today is conducted in a larger society that itself has been influenced by the moral and ethical expectations of Jewish and Christian traditions. Therefore, there is a kind of restraint in the cultural context of the church in the fact that there exists a norm of acceptable behavior, vaguely defined though it is. Not so for Gentile Christians of the first century.

Second, religions from which many converts came did not join the practice of religion and morality as is assumed in Judaism and Christianity. To be expected to do so in the church was for them new, strange, difficult. If anyone encouraged keeping the old lifestyle while embracing the new religion, no doubt many would find the combination to their liking. Paul's letters to the church in Corinth reveal a number of ways in which prebaptismal habits infected postbaptismal lives.

The Opponents' Fall from Grace (2 Peter 2:20–22)

2:20 **For if, after they have escaped the defilements of the world through the knowledge of our Lord and Savior Jesus Christ, they are again entangled in them and overpowered, the last state has become worse for them than the first.** 21 **For it would have been better for them never to have known the way of righteousness than, after knowing it, to turn back from the holy commandment that was passed on to them.** 22 **It has happened to them according to the true proverb,**

    "The dog turns back to its own vomit,"

and,

    "The sow is washed only to wallow in the mud."

Jesus told a story of a person who had an unclean spirit exorcised. The spirit wandered homeless and then decided to return to the person from whom it had been expelled. Finding seven other spirits to join it, the unclean spirit returned to a life now empty, clean, and in order. The eight moved in and the last state was worse than the first (Matt. 12:43–45). This story must have been in the mind of the writer of 2:20–22. In addition, supporting proverbs about the filthy ways of dogs (Prov. 26:11) and hogs (obviously a non-Jewish saying) return the writer to the opening sentences of the description of these heretics: they are like animals in their behavior.

The stern and even harsh conclusion to chapter 2 is unsurpassed in the New Testament, but not without its companion texts. Jesus spoke of some acts so contradictory to God's will that it would have been better if the perpetrator had been dropped into the sea with a millstone tied to the neck

(Mark 9:42–43) or even never been born at all (Mark 14:21). The epistle to the Hebrews, struggling like 2 Peter with the seriousness of turning back from Christ to one's former life, is no less sober in its assessment:

> For it is impossible to restore again to repentance those who have once been enlightened, and have tasted the heavenly gift, and have shared in the Holy Spirit, and have tasted the goodness of the word of God and the powers of the age to come, and then have fallen away, since on their own they are crucifying again the Son of God and holding him up to contempt (Heb. 6:4–6).

For centuries the church struggled with the sin of turning back from faith and with the possibility of a second repentance for backsliders, but never with more gravity than is found in 2 Peter 2:20–22.

THE FAREWELL ADDRESS: RETURN TO THE ISSUE OF THE LORD'S COMING
2 Peter 3:1–16

Thorny as the issue of the second coming is, for both early and modern Christians, it is refreshing to return to it after the lengthy attack on the false teachers. Let us remind ourselves, the issue was stated in 1:16: "The power and coming of our Lord Jesus Christ." There followed brief arguments in support of the truth of this doctrine. Then in what I called a rhetorical rampage, the writer attacked, exposed, and placed under God's judgment those who denied the second coming of Christ. Let us not forget the motivation for Christian living has many springs, and the New Testament clearly testifies to that. One of those feeding springs is the doctrine of Christ's return, with reward and punishment to follow. For 2 Peter this is *the* prime motivation. This feeds, fuels, and impels the Christian life. For certain teachers in the church to deny it, to disparage it, to scoff at the idea, is for the writer of 2 Peter a monumental sin with results catastrophic for the life and faith of the church. Given the author's premise about the centrality of this teaching, his passionate speech and his fear for the church are understandable. One could wish that those who find elsewhere in the gospel the primary motivation for Christian living would be no less passionate in their witness and no less concerned for the future of the church.

And so the writer returns to debate the doctrine with his opponents, with reason now somewhat cooler and with clarity as to what the teaching means in the life of the listening church.

The Message Stated (2 Peter 3:1–2)

> 3:1 **This is now, beloved, the second letter I am writing to you; in them I am trying to arouse your sincere intention by reminding you** ² **that you should remember the words spoken in the past by the holy prophets, and the commandment of the Lord and Savior spoken through your apostles.**

By resuming the stated purpose of reminding the readers of what they have been taught, the writer again picks up the thread of 1:12–16. Apparently there is no felt need to repeat 1:16; the readers know that the coming of the Lord is the subject solidly fixed in the unbroken tradition of prophets, Jesus, and apostles. The phrase "through your apostles" is hardly what one of the apostles would say. We are reading a letter of a later-generation disciple of Simon Peter. The reference to a prior letter may be to 1 Peter since the two epistles have some things in common. However, 1 Peter is to churches facing entirely different problems, and the writer's appeal is not to an apostolic tradition but to the example of the suffering Jesus. New situations call for new accents from the gospel, but we must be open to the possibility that 2 Peter 3:1 points to a previous letter to which we have no access.

The Message Argued (2 Peter 3:3–10)

> 3:3 **First of all you must understand this, that in the last days scoffers will come, scoffing and indulging their own lusts** ⁴ **and saying, "Where is the promise of his coming? For ever since our ancestors died, all things continue as they were from the beginning of creation!"** ⁵ **They deliberately ignore this fact, that by the word of God heavens existed long ago and an earth was formed out of water and by means of water,** ⁶ **through which the world of that time was deluged with water and perished.** ⁷ **But by the same word the present heavens and earth have been reserved for fire, being kept until the day of judgment and destruction of the godless.**
> ⁸ **But do not ignore this one fact, beloved, that with the Lord one day is like a thousand years, and a thousand years are like one day.** ⁹ **The Lord is not slow about his promise, as some think of slowness, but is patient with you, not wanting any to perish, but all to come to repentance.** ¹⁰ **But the day of the Lord will come like a thief, and then the heavens will pass away with a loud noise, and the elements will be dissolved with fire, and the earth and everything that is done on it will be disclosed.**

Recall from our earlier discussions that a major component of a farewell address is the prediction of troubles for the followers once the leader is dead. Here in this section that trouble for the church of 2 Peter comes into clearest focus: scoffers will appear, saying, "Where is the promise of his coming? For ever since our ancestors died, all things continue as they were from the beginning of creation!" (v. 4). Do not be surprised by their presence, says the writer, they are one of the signs of the last days. And do not think, says the author, that their position on this issue has been reached through prayerful study; their rejection of this teaching is born of sinful lust. In other words, they wish to continue a lifestyle best served by a denial of the Lord's coming. This is not to say that the argument of the adversaries lacks an intellectual component. They make a reasonable case.

And what is their case? Just this: With reference to the specific doctrine of the Lord's return, our forebears expected that event within their lifetimes. They were confident that it had been promised (Matt. 10:23; Mark 9:1; 1 Cor. 7:29–31). But generations come and go, and nothing has happened. Some tenacious believers hold on to the expectation, but even they have replaced the cardboard sign hand-lettered "Jesus is coming soon" with one made of concrete and steel. The words are there, but the conviction is gone. And some in the church of 2 Peter now insist the words not be said anymore. They prefer to scoff at the idea of the second coming rather than be embarrassed by it. We must not, of course, think that this is a problem unique to this church. Paul had already addressed a question in Thessalonica (1 Thess. 4:13–18): Christ has not returned yet and some of our members have died; what happens to them? Mark warned against false claims that Christ had returned. The gospel, he said, must first be preached to all nations (13:10). Matthew dealt with the delay of Christ's return in a series of parables about employers returning later than expected and a bridegroom not arriving until midnight (Matthew 24—25). And John sometimes gives the impression that the presence of the Holy Spirit is the returned Christ (14:18–16:16). But here in 2 Peter, rather than reinterpret the second coming, the scoffers disparage the whole idea.

It is evident, however, that with the adversaries the doctrine of the Lord's return is but a specific element in a larger pattern of cynical skepticism. There is no evidence, they say, that God ever intervenes in the life of the world, either in providence or in judgment. Life is one uninterrupted continuity from creation until now, so do not look to heaven for rescue or punishment. It has not come; it will not come. Not that the adversaries have been looking and have been disappointed. Faith that does believe in the providence and in the final triumph of God experiences disappointment and delay. But in the writer's view, these opponents are now jaded and cynical and do not seek the return of Christ. It would disrupt their indulgences. Apparently the scoffers have bought into one of the current philosophies that saw the world and life as a cycle, going nowhere, much like one finds in the melancholy musings of Ecclesiastes.

But, says the writer, the heretics ignore three facts, and they do so deliberately. Fact number one: the word of God (vv. 5–7). By the power of God's word the heavens and the earth were created. By that same word the world was destroyed. It has happened, and it will happen, but next time not by water but by fire. That there would be a final universal holocaust was a belief rather widely held in late Judaism as is evident in apocalyptic literature, including documents found among the Dead Sea Scrolls. Many Jews, Christians, and subscribers to other religions believed in a fiery place of punishment for the wicked, but 2 Peter also registers belief in an all-consuming fire accompanying the return of Christ. That fire will dissolve the heavens and will disclose all that has been done on earth, both good and evil.

The second fact that the scoffers ignore is the difference between God's time and human time (v. 8). Judgment is God's business and will be accomplished on God's schedule. That which we experience as a long delay should be regarded from another perspective. Using Psalm 90:4, the writer says "with the Lord one day is like a thousand years, and a thousand years are like one day."

The third and final fact ignored by the adversaries is the character of God (v. 9). Throughout the Bible God is portrayed as patient and long-suffering, giving wrongdoers second chances. Time and again Israel received this benefit, and so did the wicked Nineveh to which Jonah was sent to preach destruction. But the people repented, and God repented, and Jonah was angry. "I knew that you are a gracious God and merciful, slow to anger, and abounding in steadfast love, and ready to relent from punishing" (Jonah 4:2). God continues to be "patient with you, not wanting any to perish, but all come to repentance" (2 Peter 3:9). And so, rather than being cynical and scoffing, let the whole church express gratitude to God for what seems a delay but what is in reality a demonstration of God's patient grace. With these lines of argument, the writer concludes his attempt to silence the adversaries and rehabilitate the doctrine of the Lord's coming.

The Message Applied (2 Peter 3:11–15a)

3:11 **Since all these things are to be dissolved in this way, what sort of persons ought you to be in leading lives of holiness and godliness, ^{12} waiting for and hastening the coming of the day of God, because of which the heav-**

ens will be set ablaze and dissolved, and the elements will melt with fire? [13] **But, in accordance with his promise, we wait for new heavens and a new earth, where righteousness is at home.**

[14] **Therefore, beloved, while you are waiting for these things, strive to be found by him at peace, without spot or blemish;** [15] **and regard the patience of our Lord as salvation.**

As stated several times earlier, the author is not engaged in a classroom disagreement over an item in the church's creed: "From thence he shall come to judge the living and the dead." Doctrine is joined to behavior. Those who have mocked this teaching have openly flaunted a libertine way of life, and the author is persuaded there is a connection between their views and their values. So it is to be with the believers who hold fast to this doctrine: Faith will show itself in quality of life. The transient nature of all created things should prompt a stronger hold on the Creator. The coming dissolution of heaven and earth should effect in believers renewed attachment to that which is eternal. And the anticipation of a new heaven and a new earth (Isa. 65:17; Rev. 21:1) should have in the church a sanctifying influence. How refreshing verse 13 is! After lengthy arguments with the heretics and vivid warnings of the fire next time, the writer turns in pastoral care toward those still clutching the promise of something better and asks that they match God's patience (v. 9) with their own. Wait, he says; there will be a new time and place "where righteousness is at home."

That promise has kept alive small rural churches without adequate leadership, inner city churches surrounded by violence and burning with anger over injustice, and comfortable suburban churches who eat well but are still hungry. And this is not to mention the countless individual believers who find every day a hundred reasons for joining the scoffers but who continue to believe the promise one more day. For one more day life will be marked by peace, integrity, a refusal to sink into dissipation, and a conviction that God's delays mean continued opportunity for more embrace of forgiving grace.

The Message Supported by Paul (2 Peter 3:15b–16)

3:15b **So also our beloved brother Paul wrote to you according to the wisdom given him,** [16] **speaking of this as he does in all his letters. There are some things in them hard to understand, which the ignorant and unstable twist to their own destruction, as they do the other scriptures.**

Essentially the message to the readers is concluded, but it is important for the writer to add as a closing word that Paul agrees with what has been said. Paul is "our beloved brother," reflecting a relationship far different from that portrayed in Gal. 2:11–14 where Paul recalls a clash between himself and Peter. But this letter belongs to a later time. Peter is dead, Paul is dead, and Paul's letters (how many?) have been collected from the widely scattered churches to which he wrote, are being circulated among churches to which they were not originally addressed, and are being read as scripture. From this distance the apostolic era is viewed with idealism, as a kind of Camelot, a time when with one voice the apostles of Jesus gave to the church the normative tradition, a time prior to the arrival of false teachers and scoffers.

Yes, says the writer, Peter and Paul agree. And they do agree on the coming day of the Lord and the need for a life of godliness in view of that coming day (1 Cor. 1:7–8; Phil. 1:10; 1 Thess. 3:13; 5:23). They agree also that the patient forbearance of God provides time and incentive for repentance (Rom. 2:4). But Paul is introduced here for another reason, for if confirmation of the message of 2 Peter were the sole purpose, that has been covered at 3:2: Prophets, Jesus, and apostles all agree. Paul is singled out here because his letters are being used by the adversaries in support of their position. What possibly could they find in Paul to advance their own doctrine or ethics? Two possibilities come to mind. One, Paul did teach that in Christ we have died to sin and have been raised to new life (Rom. 6:1–11). Such statements, if removed from Paul's clear affirmations about the day of the Lord, could be twisted to mean that the time we believe in Christ is the end of the age and the beginning of the new, and, therefore, there is to be no further judgment or coming of the Lord. Two, Paul preached freedom from the law, from sin, from death (Romans 5—8). "For freedom Christ has set us free. Stand firm, therefore, and do not submit again to a yoke of slavery" (Gal. 5:1). If one stops there and does not listen to Paul's second word: "only do not use your freedom as an opportunity for self-indulgence" (Gal. 5:13), then Paul can be quoted as the champion of all kinds of "freedom." Since the false teachers of 2 Peter promised their followers freedom (2:19), this may have been the point at which they quoted Paul. And the author here is right: Given the range of issues Paul addressed, his often complicated style of argumentation, and the occasional nature of his letters, "there are some things in them hard to understand" (3:16).

CLOSING WORDS
2 Peter 3:17–18

3:17 **You therefore, beloved, since you are forewarned, beware that you are not carried away with the error of the lawless and lose your own stabil-**

ity. [18] **But grow in the grace and knowledge of our Lord and Savior Jesus Christ. To him be the glory both now and to the day of eternity. Amen.**

The shift from the valedictory address is hardly noticeable because the closing is lacking in some of the features we have come to associate with Paul's letters. No companions of the writer send greetings, and no persons among those addressed are singled out with a special word. But given the general nature of the letter's address (1:1), this ending is not surprising. The "beloved" appearing here and several times previously does not reveal a particularly close relationship between the writer and the readers. It was a literary commonplace, much like "dear" in "Dear Mrs. Brown."

The closing contains three elements. First, a reminder: You have now been adequately forewarned, so there is no reason to be swept off your feet by these permissive voices. You have been firmly grounded; stay there. Second, get on with your Christian lives. Avail yourselves of all the resources that make for growth in grace and in knowledge (note the return to the introductory accent on knowledge, 1:3). Without growth in faith, one remains immature and unstable, an easy target for anyone quoting scripture and promising freedom. And finally, the doxology to Christ: "To him be the glory both now and to the day of eternity" sends the mind back over the letter to recall the Christ of 2 Peter. He is not the ethical example in whose steps we are to walk. He is not the suffering Christ who shows us how to take abuse without retaliating. He is not the Christ of the cross, bearing our sins. He is the ascended, exalted Christ who, in God's good time, will return to end the reign of evil and usher in the new age, "where righteousness is at home."

A FINAL WORD

Now that we have read 2 Peter together, let me make three comments about its central teaching, around which clustered many other issues: the coming of Christ. First, notice with what restraint the doctrine is presented. Popular preaching and writing on the subject have often mixed into one grand image an undifferentiated collection of texts from both testaments, plus traditional notions of heaven and hell, together with unchastened imagination aimed at fears of death and the hereafter. Beside such multimedia presentations, 2 Peter is quite subdued.

Second, let this letter provide the occasion for coming clear to ourselves what we believe on the subject. It is easy enough to be reactive in one's beliefs: I do not believe in evangelism because of the fraud of tele-vangelists. I do not believe in charitable endeavors because some recipients are ne'er-do-wells. I do not believe in the hereafter because some preachers try to scare their listeners. Having said that, What do I believe? What is my vision of the end of history? To what goal or purpose does life move?

And finally, reflect on the coming of Christ in ways that are larger than the single theme of a "second" coming. The New Testament amply testifies to the coming or presence of Christ in many ways and on many occasions. The time between Christ's resurrection and the final triumph of God is not for the church a long season of the absence of Christ. In fact, one of the oldest and most enduring images of God is that of "the One who comes to us." If we set 2 Peter's focus on the final coming into this larger frame of reference, we can better appreciate the church's reading of 2 Peter 3 during the Advent season.

Jude

Introduction

In the recent past, at a large assembly of Christians, a powerful and moving sermon was preached by a relatively unknown pastor. The text of the sermon was the epistle of Jude. Afterward a pulpiteer of national repute observed, "I have never before heard a sermon on Jude. I know I have never preached one." A striking but not surprising comment. After all, not a verse from Jude appears in the Revised Common Lectionary. But then it is a very brief letter following two very brief letters, 2 and 3 John. And Jude is buried near the end of the New Testament, its very location saying to the church, "After the Gospels, Acts, letters of Paul, and Hebrews, you may continue to read if you wish, but it is not necessary." Immediately after Jude lies Revelation, and this small document of 25 verses is hardly a barrier between the reader and the terrible splendor of that intimidating book. The reader who happens upon Jude looks past it to the glow and disturbing sounds of the Apocalypse just beyond and cautiously backs away into the more familiar land of Jesus' stories and Paul's journeys.

However, the one who pauses long enough to read Jude may find more delight than dread, more familiarity than strangeness. Of course, those of us who have recently read 2 Peter will find ourselves most at home. When we come to Jude 6–19, names, places, phrases, and the flow of the argument will be recognized. For example:

2 Peter 2:4	Jude 6
For if God did not spare the angels when they sinned, but cast them into hell and committed them to chains of deepest darkness to be kept until the judgment . . .	And the angels who did not keep their own position, but left their proper dwelling, he has kept in eternal chains in deepest darkness for the judgment of the great Day.

This and other even more striking parallels between Jude and 2 Peter 2 will compel us to deal with the twin questions: Why are they so similar? Why are they different? We will for the present delay those questions. In fact, we will approach Jude as though we had not recently read 2 Peter and walk around in this small book looking for any sign that will make us feel sufficiently at home to want to stay awhile.

WHAT WE ALREADY KNOW

It is a pleasant surprise to walk into a strange room and immediately recognize a number of people. Besides Jesus Christ, there are Moses (v. 9); Enoch (v. 14), the ancient saint who went to God without experiencing death (Gen. 5:21–24); Adam (v. 14), ancestor of us all; and Cain (v. 11) who killed his brother Abel. We probably would not remember Balaam (v. 11) were it not for the talking jackass that he rode (Numbers 22—24). Korah (v. 11) is not remembered, but the fact that he was a rebel makes us want to know against what or whom (Numbers 16). We recall an archangel, Gabriel, from Luke's Christmas story but not Michael (v. 9) even though he appears in both testaments (Dan. 10:13, 21; 12:1; Rev. 12:7). Our difficulty with the brothers Jude and James (v. 1) is that we have met so many persons in the New Testament with those names. Two of the twelve apostles were named Jude (Luke 6:14–16; the name is Judas, but after the betrayal by Judas Iscariot, Jude sounds better). Jesus had a brother named Jude (Mark 6:3), and an outstanding prophet in the early church bore this name (Acts 15:22–33). As for James, we remember meeting a brother of Jesus by that name (Gal. 1:19; 2:9), and a James, son of Alphaeus, who was one of the twelve (Luke 6:15), and James, son of Zebedee and brother of John, also an apostle and close friend of Jesus (Luke 6:14; 9:28). But since this Jude and James are brothers, then they must be two of Jesus' four brothers (Mark 6:3). If so, then why not identify himself as Jude, brother of Jesus? Or maybe this is a different Jude. The name was quite common.

As for places only three are mentioned. They are all familiar but not favorably regarded in scripture. Egypt (v. 5) was for Israel the land of bondage (Exodus 1) and for the holy family a place to hide the infant Jesus from King Herod (Matt. 2:13–21). And, of course, Sodom and Gomorrah (v. 7) came to symbolize cities harboring the worst sinners and grossest evil (Genesis 19).

Perhaps most pleasantly surprising, however, has been listening to Jude and hearing words and phrases and ideas that trigger recognition. Of course, no one with any respectable record of church attendance has not heard about the coming of the Lord (v. 14) and eternal fire (v. 7). However, many of us have heard church fellowship dinners and the Eucharist referred to as "love feasts" without knowing the term came from Jude (v. 12). In fact, those who used the expression may not have known. And praying in the Holy Spirit (v. 20) is familiar, perhaps not so much because similar phrases are found elsewhere in the New Testament (Rom. 8:26; 1 Cor. 14:15; Eph. 5:18) but because the expression is used often in charismatic movements that have flourished in the last twenty years. Among those whose religious experiences have included hearing evangelistic preaching, there will be some recognition of Jude 23: "save others by snatching them out of the fire." The expression gained currency as a way of referring to last-minute or deathbed conversions. Parallel phrases from the evangelists praised the quick effectiveness of God's grace as being able to save "between the bridge and the water" or "between the stirrup and the ground." Not infrequently one hears from Sunday pulpits of "the faith that was once for all entrusted to the saints" (v. 3). But perhaps most familiar of all is the beautiful benediction that moved from Jude 24–25 into the liturgy of the church and into the memory of ministers who lift their hands over the worshipers and close the service by saying:

> Now to him who is able to keep you from falling, and to make you stand without blemish in the presence of his glory with rejoicing, to the only God our Savior, through Jesus Christ our Lord, be glory, majesty, power, and authority, before all time and now and forever. Amen.

WHAT WE WISH TO KNOW

Who is Jesus Christ as portrayed in this book? This question emerges early or late, whether one approaches scripture with faith seeking understanding or with understanding seeking faith. The question can, of course, be too preoccupying, causing the reader to press the texts to say what they do not say and in the process miss other matters of importance. But even so, for those for whom Christ is the "canon within the canon," it is fair to ask a text to yield some contribution to the multifaceted presentation of Jesus Christ in the New Testament.

The search seems at first disappointing. The titles we have heard elsewhere occur here: Master and Lord (v. 4). The expression "Lord Jesus

Christ" here is used as though in the church that is his name (vv. 4, 17, 21, 25). That the Lord is coming again is not an original contribution, but Jude does confirm it in an unusual way. A prophecy in a noncanonical book, *1 Enoch*, which originally referred to God's coming with ten thousands of the holy ones, is here applied to Christ (vv. 14–15). That prophecy, heavy with judgment on the ungodly, is balanced, however, with the hopeful word to the believers: "look forward to the mercy of our Lord Jesus Christ that leads to eternal life" (v. 21).

One noticeable accent on God's work in Christ is that of being kept safe and secure from falling (vv. 1, 24) although some responsibility for remaining in grace rests with the believers (vv. 20–21). The expression that the NRSV translates "kept safe for Jesus Christ" (v. 1) is difficult to understand with certainty. It may also be translated "by" or "in" Jesus Christ. The NEB borrows help from 1 Thess. 5:23 and renders the phrase "kept safe for the coming of Jesus Christ." As for the historical Jesus who preached, taught, healed, and went about doing good, there is no mention except that he had apostles (v. 17). The readers know God's call and gracious salvation, but any reference to its having been accomplished on the cross is noticeably absent. The resurrection of Christ is present only by implication in the doctrine of the Lord's coming.

But these silences are not in and of themselves indicting. The prior and continuing relationship between the writer and the readers and the emergency situation of the church dictate that not everything believed about Jesus Christ need be recited in this brief letter. A note from a sister in a distant city containing little more than a recipe for pumpkin pie contains much more than a recipe for pumpkin pie. Timing and appropriateness count for something. One wearies of those persons who are everywhere and all the time verbalizing everything they believe to everyone. We should concede that those to whom this letter was sent heard more than do we to whom the letter was not intended. The writer assumes the readers have been thoroughly instructed in the faith (v. 5). The instruction obviously included the teaching of the apostles (v. 17), the Old Testament (vv. 5–11), and writings from late Judaism not in the Old Testament (vv. 9, 14–15). The author was in the process of preparing correspondence "about the salvation we share" (v. 3) when news came of dangerous and divisive intruders stealing into the church. As a consequence, this letter is quickly written and posted to warn, to urge, to encourage the addressees. What the originally planned letter would have contained we could only begin to guess.

What, then, is it to be Christian in the time and place of the recipients of this epistle? Not everything said to them is directly portable to us, of course, but this is the way we learn. After all, we are more alike than different. In the church of Jude, to be Christian is to share with other believers in the love feasts and, by implication, to participate in the worship assemblies of the congregation. It is to stand firm in the faith, drawing upon the full instruction in the tradition that probably came prior to the time of baptism. To be Christian is to contend for that faith, not being intimidated or beguiled by either the bombastic or the flattering speech of the worldly wise intruders (vv. 16, 19). It is to realize one's own vulnerability and capacity for going astray and therefore, to be diligent in prayer, in keeping oneself within the circle of love that flows from God, in strengthening faith through all available resources, and in constant hope of Christ's mercy. And to be Christian means that those who throw themselves on Christ's mercy will themselves be merciful in their attention to the weak, the faltering, and those trapped in the web of evil, knowing how easily helpers can slip into playing God or the devil. One must never overestimate one's own spiritual strength, says Jude. Have mercy "with fear" (v. 23).

A WAY TO BEGIN

As with 1 and 2 Peter, we begin commenting on Jude from a perspective based on four tentative but not unsupported affirmations about the book.

What Kind of Literature Is It?

Jude is a letter. Not all the features of a first-century letter are present, but the opening and closing make it clear the writer wanted it to be so regarded. Jude certainly has more epistolary traits than Hebrews or 1 John. And Jude is classified as a general letter because its recipients are not identified by time or place, but this is *our* classification. "Those who are called, who are beloved in God the Father and kept safe for Jesus Christ" (v. 1) may have been a congregation of believers who knew the letter was for them and them alone. It is not the epistle the author was intending to write, but in spite of its brevity and single-issue focus, Jude has literary grace. It is written in a style dignified and at times poetic. We will have occasion to note these qualities as we go.

We will also observe the literary relationship between Jude and 2 Peter 2. Most scholars argue for 2 Peter's dependence on Jude, but the reverse is possible, as is also their drawing on a common source. Settling that issue, even if we could, would help us very little in understanding Jude, and so our primary energies will be spent in listening to what this text has to say.

Who Wrote the Letter?

We do not know. It is written by, or offered in the name of (in the tradition of) one Jude, "a servant of Jesus Christ and brother of James." To identify oneself as a brother of James implies that James is prominent in the church. From our records this would mean James the brother of Jesus (Acts 15; Galatians 2). And this James had a brother Jude (Mark 6:3), both being brothers of Jesus. It seemed more appropriate to Christian leadership not to claim that relation to Jesus but rather to be identified as servant of Jesus, brother of James. Those who attribute the letter to Jude the brother of James and Jesus date it as one of the early writings of the New Testament and place it in a Palestinian Jewish Christian context. To say it is the work of a disciple of Jude in this particular circle of Christianity suggests a later date and perhaps even a location beyond the birth land of the church. The exhortation to "remember the predictions of the apostles of our Lord Jesus Christ" (v. 17) certainly sounds like the words of a postapostolic writer.

To Whom Was the Letter Written?

We do not know. Earlier in this Introduction an attempt was made to identify the readers from the sketchy evidence within the letter itself. Nothing of substance can be added here except the warning that our classification of Jude as one of the seven general epistles does not justify the conclusion the letter was therefore to Christians everywhere or was a circular letter to be passed among the churches. The address on the letter does not say Yes or No to such theories.

For What Purpose Was the Letter Written?

We accept as the purpose of this letter what the content rather clearly reveals: that is, to alert the church to the intruders among them who pervert the faith and divide the faithful, and to exhort the believers to stand firm in faith, to grow in grace, and to be renewed in the mercy that Christ shows toward them and that they are to exhibit toward those who falter and fail. The doctrinal error of the troublemakers is not evident; their licentious lifestyle is the real threat. That they deny Christ (v. 4) is not a christological position but refers to their conduct. They may have made false claims about the Holy Spirit (vv. 19, 20) and seem to flaunt an independence that disregards the health of the community (v. 12). There have always been souls among the faithful fascinated by and drawn to such leaders, especially if they are articulate and passionate (v. 16). Jude knows that; hence the letter.

OUTLINE OF JUDE

Letters, by their very nature, do not yield easily to outlines. For purposes of order and clarity, however, the commentary to follow will be structured on this sketch of the contents:

Salutation   1–2
Occasion of the Letter   3–4
Lessons from History   5–7
Indictment of the Intruders   8–13
Lessons from Prophecy   14–19
Closing Appeal   20–23
Concluding Doxology   24–25

Commentary

SALUTATION
Jude 1–2

¹ **Jude, a servant of Jesus Christ and brother of James,**
  To those who are called, who are beloved in God the Father and kept safe
  for Jesus Christ:
  ² **May mercy, peace, and love be yours in abundance.**

In the Introduction we discussed the names "Jude" and "James." Little more
need be or can be said here. It is worth noting, however, that "a servant of
Jesus Christ" was not for the author sufficient identification and so "brother
of James" is added. Why so? With Paul and others the relationship to Jesus
Christ was enough; to list other connections was unnecessary. Perhaps this
letter is sent into a Christian circle where the writer is not a recognized authority but his brother James is. In my judgment adding the name of James
is further evidence (see v. 17) that this letter is from the postapostolic era. For
the apostles, their relation to Christ authorized their ministries. With the
passing of the apostles, one had to establish one's connections with the tradition in order to be heard as a representative of the truth from Jesus,
through the apostles, to the church. James is that connection. Furthermore,
one cannot miss what the writer only indirectly says: I am a brother of Jesus'
brother; in other words, I am servant (but also brother) of Jesus.

The addressees are identified not geographically but theologically; that
is, they are located in relation to God's activity toward them. That activity is expressed in three words that imply at least what God has done, is
doing, and will do: God has called or chosen them; God is holding them
in the constancy of divine love; God will keep them safe, will guard them
securely for the coming of Jesus Christ. The image is one of stability, quite
the opposite of the intruders who are "clouds carried along by the winds"
and "wandering stars" (vv. 12, 13).

The threefold greeting seems more tailored for the occasion than standardized for general use. "Mercy" reappears three times in the closing appeal (vv. 21–23). Peace is longed for in a situation plagued by grumblers, malcontents, and schismatics (vv. 16, 19). And the love of God is the dwelling place of the believers (vv. 1, 21). The greeting, then, is more than a greeting; even in its brevity it anticipates the affirmation, the polemic, and the exhortation in the body of the letter.

OCCASION OF THE LETTER
Jude 3–4

³ **Beloved, while eagerly preparing to write to you about the salvation we share, I find it necessary to write and appeal to you to contend for the faith that was once for all entrusted to the saints.** ⁴ **For certain intruders have stolen in among you, people who long ago were designated for this condemnation as ungodly, who pervert the grace of our God into licentiousness and deny our only Master and Lord, Jesus Christ.**

Following the greeting, the reader of a letter of that time and place expects either a burst of thanksgiving (as in Phil. 1:3–11) or a lengthy eulogy in praise of God (as in 1 Peter 1:3–12). But not this time, and understandably so. The church addressed is experiencing a crisis. Recall that the only letter of Paul containing neither thanksgiving nor eulogy is Galatians. That letter reflects a crisis in the churches of Galatia that both hurt and incensed Paul. Here, too, a problem of major proportions needs attention. The writer is not as emotional as Paul but does feel the obligation to respond. Apparently the author was preparing a letter affirming and celebrating their common salvation, a letter more deliberately framed and not issue-driven. Then the news about the intruders came, and that long-planned letter had to be delayed in order to dash off this urgent note.

That these intruders "have stolen in" is no criticism of the church. The leaders could have been on duty keeping sentinel watch over the flock. This sort of thing happens all the time, and the reasons are several. Church folk live in and by trust and are, therefore, vulnerable. However, a church that hardens into suspicion may keep out intruders, but sincere seekers are often shut out as well. Churches practice hospitality to strangers, or should, but strangers pose a threat. A policeman guarding the door may protect those inside, but they cease to be a church. Churches are open to new understandings of God's ways in the world, or should be, but openness is unsettling. One can shut down discussion, but in the false peace that follows a prophet may be silenced or the Spirit quenched. And religion is easily counterfeited. Its rituals, its language, its intangible essentials can be mimicked by the clever, and soon the damage is done. "Christ has set you free," they said, "free from moral restraints." By so living and teaching, says the writer, they deny Christ. In their mouths the grace of God is cheapened into permissiveness, perhaps much as Paul met in those who twisted his sermons on grace to imply that we continue in sin so that grace might abound (Romans 6).

This sudden and hastily prepared letter was not intended to alarm the church as though some new, surprising, and deadly problem were threatening the very purpose of God. People such as these intruders appeared in prophecies long before they appeared in church. The writer will soon cite a prophecy in *1 Enoch* (vv. 14–15) and subsequently predictions by the apostles (vv. 17–18). What is important at this point in the letter is to say to the readers, "Be on guard, but do not panic. Take the long view. Prophecy and fulfillment enable you to do that. In addition, prophecy and fulfillment mean things are not totally out of control. God's knowledge and purpose are still in place." This is not an uncommon view of life and God. A person in the middle of a terrible storm finds some peace in the assertion, "The Bible said things like this would happen." One can hardly imagine a disturbance greater than that created by Jesus' betrayal by a follower and friend. But the writer of the Fourth Gospel restores some order and sense by saying Judas's act fulfilled prophecy: "The one who ate my bread has lifted his heel against me" (John 13:18; Psalm 41:9). A similar effect follows from Jude's identifying the intruders as "people who long ago were designated for this condemnation" (v. 4).

In view of this recent disturbing development in the church, the appeal is clear and strong: "Contend for the faith that was once for all entrusted to the saints" (v. 3). What this assignment involves will be fleshed out in the letter itself, but two observations are in order here. First, "the faith . . . entrusted" is literally "the faith . . . traditioned." What is at stake is the central body of beliefs, the tradition. We could write disparagingly of this perspective and lament the passing of those lively first-generation days when faith was not *the* faith but was rather trust, a relationship with God through Jesus Christ. But that would be a false dichotomy. Both faith and *the* faith were present from the early days. Paul summarizes the core content of what we believe in 1 Cor. 15:1–8. Such formulations were in place quite early in the Christian mission and helpfully so. Faith is not a vague and general feeling. It has content. One cannot plant a tree on a cloud. And in the present case of Jude, contenders for the faith are also expected to love, pray, grow, hope, and demonstrate mercy toward others. Their faith is not reduced to a doctrinal dispute.

Second, to "contend" does not necessarily mean to become defensive or to be conservative in the sense of making a goal of the status quo. The verb means "to wrestle" or "to struggle." When put into English letters, the Greek word is "agonize." Paul used the word when he asked the church in Rome "to join me in earnest prayer"; that is, "agonize with me in prayer" (Rom. 15:30). Jude is asking for passionate engagement in the life of discipleship, to behave as though who God is, who Christ is, and who we are really matter. Something is at stake here.

LESSONS FROM HISTORY
Jude 5–7

> [5] Now I desire to remind you, though you are fully informed, that the Lord, who once for all saved a people out of the land of Egypt, afterward destroyed those who did not believe. [6] And the angels who did not keep their own position, but left their proper dwelling, he has kept in eternal chains in deepest darkness for the judgment of the great Day. [7] Likewise, Sodom and Gomorrah and the surrounding cities, which, in the same manner as they, indulged in sexual immorality and pursued unnatural lust, serve as an example by undergoing a punishment of eternal fire.

The first readers of Jude, having been fully instructed in Old Testament narratives as a part of their preparation for church membership, needed only brief allusions to bring home to them the lessons of those narratives. No offense, but some modern readers lacking that instruction would benefit from reading the stories in their own contexts. Otherwise the full force of these three verses will not be experienced. No moral injunctions carry more weight than those that begin, "Let me remind you." In other words, you already know what I am saying and therefore you stand before the judgment of your own mind and conscience. That this section assumes a knowledge of scripture does not tell us whether the readers were Jews or Gentiles in background. To be a Jew does not automatically mean one knows the Hebrew scriptures; to be a Gentile does not automatically mean one does not. Apparently all new Christians received instruction.

The lessons of Jude 5–7 are lessons of judgment. Second Peter 2:4–8 is strikingly similar, and pausing now to read those verses could be helpful. However, there are differences. Jude draws upon the exodus while Peter uses the flood story. Jude speaks only of judgment while Peter intersperses cases of divine rescue. Jude's reasons for God's judgment differ from Peter's. These differences are not unusual or out of order. All who listen to sermons know that the same rich biblical texts yield different lessons appropriate to time, place, and audience. If the similarity between Jude 5–7 and 2 Peter 2:4–8 raises a question, several answers are plausible. Just as most New Testament scholars believe Matthew and Luke used Mark as a source, so most believe Peter used Jude. A few hold that Jude used Peter and others, including myself, that they drew upon a common source. But none of these satisfies our primary question, What is Jude saying to his readers?

The three Old Testament stories of divine judgment indict the "intruders" (v. 4) and warn the readers of three major evils. The first lesson is from the exodus, which in the main is a story of deliverance from bondage but which also carries a dark subtheme: the punishment of those who do not trust God, who do not live by faith. Not all who were led out of Egypt entered the promised land, because between the Red Sea and the Jordan there was a wilderness. The author of Hebrews draws upon this event to warn the readers of the wilderness of disobedience and testing God (Heb. 3:7–4:2). Paul likewise reminded the Corinthians that the Israelites were "baptized" in the Red Sea and had communion in the desert, but that grand beginning did not guarantee a happy ending. The wilderness journey was marked by idolatry, sexual immorality, grumbling, and putting God to the test. The guilty fell under the judgment of God. So, says Paul, "If you think you are standing, watch out that you do not fall" (1 Cor. 10:12; the entire lesson includes vv. 1–13). Similarly, Jude says that the "once for all" deliverance from Egypt was no assurance of security for those who did not keep themselves in the love of God (v. 21).

The second lesson has to do not with unbelief but with rebellion against God. The reminder is the strange and obscure story of angels (sons of God) in Gen. 6:1–4, elaborately expanded and interpreted in the noncanonical book, *1 Enoch* (chaps. 6—8). See the comments on 2 Peter 2:4. However, in 2 Peter, the angels' offense is simply called sin, presumably that of entering into forbidden sexual alliances with women on earth. Jude charges them with not keeping "their own position," of leaving "their proper dwelling" (v. 6). There is no way to miss the appropriateness of the indictment: The intruders in the church "reject authority" (v. 8). The church, following the death of the apostles, feeling strongly the necessity of preserving the tradition, regarded as especially dangerous the refusal to respect the leadership of the church (1 Tim. 5:1, 19; Heb. 13:7). Rebellion in the church they feared would break the continuity of the tradition "once for all entrusted to the saints." Likewise, among those of us who had strong sympathy for those who rebelled against authorities in the 1960s and 1970s were some who expressed fears that fundamental values and nourishing traditions would also be lost. Jesus must also have aroused such ambivalent feelings by his teachings and dramatic actions toward customs and institutions of his day.

The third and final lesson warns against sexual immorality, a warning that draws upon the classic case of Sodom and Gomorrah (Genesis 19). That the men of Sodom and Gomorrah "pursued unnatural lust" (lit., "pursued other flesh," v. 7) involved more than homosexuality. They desired sex with the two supernatural beings who visited Lot. For Jude, what happened in Sodom and Gomorrah that brought down God's fire was similar to what happened between angels and humans in Gen. 6:1–4 that brought down God's flood. That the intruders in the church had some unhealthy fascination with angelic beings (vv. 8–9) should not go unnoticed, even though the causes and expressions of that relationship are not clear to us. It is evident in verse 8 that these disrupters are so arrogant as to blaspheme the angelic servants of God who bring God's message and execute God's judgments. In other words, they are in total rebellion against heaven. But verses 6–7 at least imply a connection or a desired connection between the troublemakers and supernatural beings by means of sex. Such a thought would not have been totally foreign to first-century ears. Fertility rites by which devotees were promised participation in the life of gods and goddesses were fairly widespread. Nor has the notion of sex as a spiritual act perished from the earth. Attaining transcendence of the soul and producing special children of God through sex with some guru are promises and practices often found in cults today.

The letter of Jude is too brief for us, if not for the first readers. His hints and allusions leave us staring unknowingly into caverns too dark and too deep. What we do know is that with these intruders into the church came ideas and activities dangerous and destructive in their consequences, but in their offer of new freedoms, also attractive and promising to the weak and unstable.

INDICTMENT OF THE INTRUDERS
Jude 8–13

8 Yet in the same way these dreamers also defile the flesh, reject authority, and slander the glorious ones. 9 But when the archangel Michael contended

with the devil and disputed about the body of Moses, he did not dare to bring a condemnation of slander against him, but said, "The Lord rebuke you!" [10] But these people slander whatever they do not understand, and they are destroyed by those things that, like irrational animals, they know by instinct. [11] Woe to them! For they go the way of Cain, and abandon themselves to Balaam's error for the sake of gain, and perish in Korah's rebellion. [12] These are blemishes on your love-feasts, while they feast with you without fear, feeding themselves. They are waterless clouds carried along by the winds; autumn trees without fruit, twice dead, uprooted; [13] wild waves of the sea, casting up the foam of their own shame; wandering stars, for whom the deepest darkness has been reserved forever.

At verse 8 the broad "if the shoe fits, wear it" judgments of verses 5–7 give way to specific finger pointing. At verses 8, 10, 12, 16, and 19 the writer uses the same expression which could be translated, "These are the ones who . . ." The phrase serves to identify, and its repetition makes it clear that one group and only one group is the focus of the indictment. How, then, is this group, until now only vaguely identified as "intruders" (v. 4) characterized?

They are dreamers. Even though dreams were respected as avenues of divine revelation (Matt. 1:20–2:20), dreamers were often portrayed in a negative light (Deut. 13:1–5; Jer. 27:9) as persons who led people astray by substituting their own imaginings and soothing wishes for the word of God. They were false prophets, held captive by their own love of praise and popularity. These intruders grant sexual license to themselves and those who follow them. They have apparently arrived at a position on Christian freedom that makes them indifferent to uses of the physical body or that prompts them to indulge the flesh as proof of freedom. They resist authority as further proof of freedom and shake the fist at heaven, insulting angels as messengers of God, keepers of moral order, and executors of God's judgment. They display an arrogance not even found among beings of a higher order.

Drawing upon a legend preserved in a little-known writing of late Judaism, *The Assumption of Moses*, the writer says that not even the archangel Michael would slander a most-deserving-of-criticism Satan but rather left all matters of judgment to God (see further comments on 2 Peter 2:11). Apparently these disturbers of the church found all divine intervention, whether as revelation or providence or judgment, to be intrusive violations of their freedom, and therefore they blasphemed the angels as agents of such interventions. But, says the writer, they are thereby showing their ignorance and their kinship with brute creatures who follow base instincts, totally oblivious to any higher order of being or quality of living. It seems to be possible, although difficult to imagine, for a human being to be so preoccupied with satisfying physical appetites that the other faculties of mind and heart and spirit atrophy until the image of God fades past recognition.

At this point (v. 11) the author pronounces over the intruders the prophetic "Woe to them!" —the classic form of God's judgment (Matt. 11:21–24; Rev. 8:13). Because their sins are similar, their fates will be similar to those of the infamous trio, Cain, Balaam, and Korah. Although these three were distanced from each in the Old Testament narratives (Cain, Genesis 4; Balaam, Numbers 22—24; Korah, Numbers 16), they had long been joined in the teachings of rabbis as representative of those who have no share in the world to come. They are here being regarded by the writer more by the way they were treated in rabbinic interpretation than in the actual biblical accounts of their moral failures. For example, that the intruders are going "the way of Cain" does not mean they are guilty of murder as Cain was. According to rabbinic tradition, Cain was the first heretic in that he denied the justice of God's judgment. That interpretation makes clear the appropriateness of the writer's choice of Cain as a spiritual forebear of the intruders.

The case of Balaam, used also by 2 Peter (2:15–16), is more apparently fitting. He was a prophet willing to bless or to curse as long as the money was right. His name continues to be used to label cases of preaching for profit, just as the name of Simon the magician has provided a term to identify the purchase of ecclesiastical power with money (simony, Acts 8:9–24). Few of us would boast of being totally free of Balaam's taint.

And Korah fits perfectly the description of the intruders as rebellious and resistant to authority. He revolted against the leadership of Moses and hence against God who spoke through Moses. In doing so, he became a divisive force in the covenant community, because every community has at its fringes enough members with old wounds, complaints, axes to grind, and frustrated ambitions who will give to any uprising a measure of immediate success. This is not to say that all voices raised in opposition to established leadership are thereby raised against God and to be silenced. Sometimes God speaks in the revolt. Discerning the difference takes prayerful wisdom and courage. In all three of these cases, however, history confirmed their errors and documented their fates. The intruders and all attracted to them would do well to remember and be warned.

At verse 12 the indictment shifts from Old Testament analogies to a brief but vivid description of the conduct of the troublemakers within the life of the church addressed by the letter. They are, we must remember, members of the Christian community, and therefore they enjoy the full privileges of participation in the church's fellowship meals (love feasts). But they do so without reverence, behaving as though the table of the church at which Christ is host is no different from any table in any mess hall or public eating room. At the table fellowship they are "blemishes" (NRSV here and at 2 Peter 2:13). What does that mean? The NEB translates the word "ugly blots" at 2 Peter 2:13 and "dangers" at Jude 12. Another possible rendering is "spots," giving an image not unlike a rotten apple in a barrel of good apples. The threat to the health of the whole group is obvious. Interestingly, the term is sometimes translated "rocks" or "reefs" such as pose an immediate danger to a ship.

The images differ in the translations, but the problem remains the same. The presence of loud, irreverent revelers at the table of the church is not merely distracting. It is dangerous to the health of the fellowship. The expression "feeding themselves" (v. 12) means literally "shepherding themselves." Perhaps the intruders were not only members of the church but claimed to be pastors, that is, shepherds. If so, this would have made it even easier for them to insinuate themselves into the trust of the congregation. Churches tend to believe pastors until the pastor speaks or acts so as to shatter that confidence. But these intruders, instead of feeding and caring for the flock, feed and care only for themselves, and in so doing, reject the leadership of the church's true pastors. My mother once corrected me by saying, "We do not speak critically of our pastor or our physician." A wholesome thought, and generally speaking, good advice to a child concerning not only pastors and physicians but all who seek to help others. She was not naive but of the strong opinion that it is better to trust and then, if that trust is violated, to be surprised and disappointed than to be suspicious from the beginning. If the writer of Jude is only half right in portraying the intruders, they would have been to my mother a surprise and a disappointment.

The indictment concludes with four analogies from the world of nature. It was believed by many that, in the last days, part of the agony to precede the arrival of the Son of Man would be the results of creation gone awry (see, for example, 1 Enoch 80:2–6). The usual dependable order of things would be convoluted, times and seasons would be askew, and normal expectations disappointed. Christian writers shared such beliefs and spoke of darkness at noon, sun and moon refusing to shine, rocks splitting and mountains falling. By describing the disturbers as drifting clouds without rain, autumn trees without fruit, stormy waves polluting with filthy foam, and stars off course, the writer not only indicts them in picturesque language but also indirectly announces that these are the last days. This announcement will be made more directly in verse 18.

LESSONS FROM PROPHECY
Jude 14–19

14 It was also about these that Enoch, in the seventh generation from Adam, prophesied, saying, "See, the Lord is coming with ten thousands of his holy ones, 15 to execute judgment on all, and to convict everyone of all the deeds of ungodliness that they have committed in such an ungodly way, and of all the harsh things that ungodly sinners have spoken against him." 16 These are grumblers and malcontents; they indulge their own lusts; they are bombastic in speech, flattering people to their own advantage.

17 But you, beloved, must remember the predictions of the apostles of our Lord Jesus Christ; 18 for they said to you, "In the last time there will be scoffers, indulging their own ungodly lusts." 19 It is these worldly people, devoid of the Spirit, who are causing divisions.

This portion of the letter consists of two units that are completely parallel. Each unit consists of a prophecy from the past followed by a statement that identifies the intruders as the ones of whom the prophecy speaks. These statements (vv. 16, 19) both begin with "These are the ones." (The identical nature of the statements is slightly obscured in the translations because we tend to think exact repetition is poor style.) Both consist of summaries of the faults of the troublemakers. Neither prophecy is found within our canon of scripture although one is from a Jewish source and the other from a Christian tradition, either oral or written. We need to remember, however, that Jude comes from a time prior to any determination of which writings were to be set apart as normative scripture and preserved as helpful, and which writings were to be rejected as damaging to faith. This is not the place to engage in a lengthy discussion of all the factors that entered into such decisions, but it is important to recall that the Jewish community did not publicly announce what constituted scripture for them until well into the Christian era, and the Christian community discussed what should be the contents of its Bible for at least two centuries beyond the date of Jude. The two prophecies before us, while coming from sources not finally regarded as scripture by either Jews or Christians, were from traditions held to be true and authoritative, and contents of both prophecies are well confirmed by writings that were finally included in the canon. In other words, we will observe in each case that the prophecies are not unusual but rather lie at the center of Jewish and Christian expectations concerning the final reign of God.

The first unit (vv. 14–16) is governed by a prophecy from *1 Enoch* 1:9 with some words and phrases from elsewhere in that book. *First Enoch* was written in the second and first centuries B.C. and is found now in collections entitled *Old Testament Pseudepigrapha*. Early Christians were especially fond of *1 Enoch*—for a number of reasons. Enoch represented early antiquity, before the gross corruption that brought on the flood. Being the seventh generation from Adam made Enoch special, seven being the perfect number. And he was a holy man: "Enoch walked with God; then he was no more, because God took him" (Gen. 5:24). Hebrews lists him as a hero of faith who had pleased God (11:5). Enoch was especially qualified, therefore, to speak of God and of God's judgment on the ungodly. In its original setting the prophecy spoke of *God's* coming (see also Deut. 33:2), but Jude has Jesus Christ in mind when he says "the Lord."

Other Christian writers also understood that it would be Christ whom God would send with a host of holy angels (Matt. 25:31; Mark 8:38; 13:26–27). In this form of the prophecy of the Lord's coming there is no mention of Christ's saving work (as in Matt. 25:31–46) but only of his execution of universal judgment on the ungodly. We can only assume Jude chose this particular statement of the second advent because the burning issue before him is the fate of those who are destroying the church. Three times the prophecy speaks of the "ungodly." The word means to be without reverence, without piety, without respect or praise for God. It fits the intruders who make a boisterous party out of the church fellowship meal. In fact, Jude uses the passage in *1 Enoch* as though it were written for these very people. They act and speak without respect for God or the community of God's faithful. Like the Israelites in the wilderness, they grumble and complain about God's providence (Exod. 15:24; 17:3) while pursuing the lifestyle of the libertine. They enter a room and take it over, talking too loud, drawing everyone's attention, and then ingratiating themselves for purposes entirely selfish.

We might wonder how persons so described could actually enter a Christian community and influence members to follow them. But we must keep in mind that Jude is looking past what the intruders appear to be to what they really are. Then what might they appear to be? Perhaps articulate leaders with charismatic personalities, preaching and modeling a new freedom of speech and relationship, and bringing a party spirit to the solemn assemblies. If they toss in complaints about tradition and laugh about sermons that are too morally serious, all the while lacing their speech with statements about love and joy, for some folk the intruders become pied pipers. And if the present leadership resists or rejects, then the newly bewitched will probably leave and start a new congregation.

The second unit (vv. 17–19) is governed by "predictions of the apostles of our Lord Jesus Christ." We do not know exactly to what predictions the writer refers: perhaps 2 Peter 3:3 or Paul's similar prophecy in Acts 20:29–30. Neither do we know at what the troublemakers are scoffing. In 2 Peter the false teachers mocked the doctrine of the Lord's return, but here we can only conclude that scoffing was the general response of the intruders to beliefs and practices held dear by the church. One gets the impression that the licentious lifestyle of the disturbers was not simply a case of living out their view of freedom but also a way of mocking those who lived under the moral demands of Christ. To the writer, at least, their indulgences were a flaunting vulgarization of all that the church held sacred. And as improbable as it may seem to us that these intruders could wield much influence among church members, they apparently were seducing some because they were creating divisions.

If there is anything more surprising than the almost irrational loyalty of some people to religious leaders, it is the fact that revelations of immorality and fraud by those leaders do not shake that loyalty. No doubt many in the church were disturbed, but the writer has already ministered pastorally to them by saying, "This unsettling turn of events is not final or fatal. The apostles predicted such mockers would arise. They are a sign of the end time. And if the scoffers are here, then the end is near, and if the end is near, so is the return of Christ, the reign of God, and life eternal." It must have been such thinking that allowed the writer to turn so quickly from the grim topic of divisive troublemakers to constructive advice to the faithful about living toward the day of Christ's mercy.

CLOSING APPEAL
Jude 20–23

> 20 But you, beloved, build yourselves up on your most holy faith: pray in the Holy Spirit, 21 keep yourselves in the love of God; look forward to the mercy of our Lord Jesus Christ that leads to eternal life. 22 And have mercy on some who are wavering, 23 save others by snatching them out of the fire; and have mercy on still others with fear, hating even the tunic defiled by their bodies.

For these four verses alone, Jude deserves more attention than the church has given it. Here is instruction in Christian living equal to any that Paul gives, and it is all the more refreshing because it is unexpected in view of the crisis caused by the intruders. One would expect here at least a final warning about the troublemakers and perhaps even a call for the church to sever all association with them. Listen to Paul speak to the church in Corinth, which seems to be tolerating a member who is living with his father's wife (1 Cor. 5:11): "I am writing to you not to associate with anyone who bears the name of brother or sister who is sexually immoral or greedy, or is an idolater, reviler, drunkard, or robber. Do not even eat with such a one." Paul does hope that such action will work to restore the erring brother (1 Cor. 5:5), but even so, notice the strong initiative to be taken by the church toward such members. Or again, "Take note of those who do not obey what we say in this letter; have nothing to do with them, so that they may be ashamed" (2 Thess. 3:14). No less strict is the discipline urged in 2 John 10–11: "Do not receive into the house or welcome anyone who comes to you and does not bring this teaching; for to welcome is to participate in the evil deeds of such a person."

Of course, cases of moral or doctrinal error differed in severity, and we may assume congregations differed in methods of dealing with them. There does, however, seem to have been a broad concern and effort to practice damage control in the churches. That effort is not lacking here in Jude, but given the description of the intruders, the advice here is marked not only by restraint but by a patient mercy. Let us look more closely now at this final appeal.

First of all, notice that the writer is again directly addressing the church faithful. From verse 5b through verse 16 the letter talked *about others*; now the message is *to you*. To talk about the intruders is not gossip but pastoral concern that alerts the flock that wolves are among them.

Second, of the seven phrases of instruction or exhortation, the first four pertain to the attention the faithful should give to their own spiritual welfare (vv. 20–21). The subject areas are faith, prayer, love, and hope. As for faith, it must be strengthened and built up; otherwise their trembling, immature faith makes them especially vulnerable to false teaching and seductive lifestyles. The writer does not elaborate on methods or resources, but surely the readers knew as well as we do what those are. Worship, both private and corporate; regular fellowship with like-minded believers; study and open discussion of the faith and its meaning for life's choices and relationships; engagement in the church's ministry in the world; witnessing to one's faith among nonbelievers; these activities build up one's faith. As for prayer, it is not only to be regular but "in the Holy Spirit." What distinguishes "in the Holy Spirit" praying? On the basis of Paul's statement that "that very Spirit intercedes with sighs too deep for words" (Rom. 8:26), some hold that prayer in the Spirit is charismatic speech or speaking in tongues. Whatever may be the meaning and value of such activity, Paul's point is that we in our weakness and sinfulness do not always know the will of God in a matter before us. We continue to pray, and with our best thinking (1 Cor. 14:15), but even then we ask that the Spirit convert our prayer into petitions and intercessions consonant with God's will. After all, the Spirit knows what is the mind of God. Our prayers are our best thoughts, hopes, and desires, expressed in our own words. How those prayers "sound" when the Holy Spirit mediates them to God is not ours to know nor to imitate. We can only trust that those are the prayers which are in Christ's name, in God's will, "in the Holy Spirit." Otherwise, prayer can be selfish and destructive. Who among us is not grateful that God has not answered some of our prayers *as we prayed them*?

The third of the four instructions for spiritual health has to do with the love of God. Here the writer surely means God's love for us, not our love for God. Certainly we are beloved of God and that love keeps us "safe for Jesus Christ" (v. 1), but for all this letter's attention to being kept secure, the writer is well aware of the present spiritual state of the intruders. They, too, were baptized and received Christian instruction, but something happened along the way. Certainly God did not cease to love them, but something was lost, either by neglect or by perversion. It is no criticism of God's love or God's grace to urge Christians to keep sentinel watch over their spiritual welfare. Paul stated this paradox beautifully: "Work out your own salvation with fear and trembling; for it is God who is at work in you, enabling you both to will and to work for his good pleasure" (Phil. 2:12–13).

The last of the four instructions for spiritual health concerns hope that looks forward to Christ's mercy, mercy that welcomes us into life eternal. We live by hope. Anticipation is not only the greatest single source of pleasure, but it empowers us for the present. Hope is not whistling in the dark; it is not postponing, saying, "Oh, well, one of these days when the Messiah comes, all these problems will disappear." On the contrary, hope stirs us to life and to important endeavors, preparing ourselves and our world for the great doxology at the final Advent of God. And that which fills us with hope rather than dread is "the mercy of our Lord Jesus Christ (v. 21)." It is the anticipation of that mercy that spawns mercy in us, and that quality, says Jude, marks all our relations with others.

Finally, then, we turn to the last three of the seven instructions in the closing appeal (vv. 22–23). These injunctions have to do with the behavior of the faithful toward brothers and sisters who have gone or who are going astray. To appreciate the importance of these two verses, it is necessary to imagine how critical to the life and witness of the church was the continuing faithfulness of its members, not to mention a group's concern for a brother or sister who moved away from the circle of God's love and grace. We are talking about a tiny minority church in a vast world of superstitions, violence, and moral decay, not an established majority with millions of members who never participate. In a church that regards 30 percent participation a good record, talk of restoring erring souls may sound a bit strange. How would we respond to the request of the pastor that we try to rescue a wandering brother or sister? "You can't be serious, Reverend. Who am I to do that? We are all backsliders to a degree. Right?"

The concerns of the early church toward wayward members were two. On the one hand, following Christ meant living under the moral and ethical demands of the gospel. The Sermon on the Mount makes that clear. The Christian faith is morally serious. Everyone is welcome, of course, but not everything goes. Standards are to be observed, and flagrant violations cannot be winked at. On the other hand, some effort at forgiveness and restoration must be made. After all, did not Christ say to forgive a brother or sister seventy times seven times? James expressed it well: "My brothers and sisters, if anyone among you wanders from the truth and is brought back by another, you should know that whoever brings back a sinner from wandering will save the sinner's soul from death and will cover a multitude of sins" (5:19–20). Not surprisingly, this double concern soon led to discussions of different kinds or weights of sin. Classifications were developed. Venial sins were pardonable, mortal sins were not. As early as the closing decades of the first century such distinctions were being made. For example:

> If you see your brother or sister committing what is not a mortal sin, you will ask, and God will give life to such a one—to those whose sin is not mortal. There is sin that is mortal; I do not say that you should pray about that. All wrongdoing is sin, but there is sin that is not mortal. (1 John 5:16–17)

One remarkable feature of Jude 22–23 is that while all sin is taken seriously, and while there is a recognition that there are differences in degrees of spiritual danger, at no point and before no case of erring are the faithful instructed to back away and withdraw their concern.

If some of you study this unit in a group where several translations are used, attention will be drawn to noticeable differences in the readings. These are not due solely to a range of ways of translating the same Greek words. The fact is, many of the Greek manuscripts (we have more than 5,000) differ in the wording of these two verses. For example, "have mercy" and "convince" translate very similar words in verse 22; some manuscripts have one, some the other. A number of you will have Bibles with a footnote after verse 23: "The Greek text is uncertain." Acknowledging that fact, we will comment on this unit as it is translated in the NRSV.

There are three groups toward whom the faithful are to show mercy in view of their own hope of the mercy of Christ. The three are presented in an order of increasing seriousness. The first group are the wavering. Doubts and uncertainties move like clouds across their faith. Perhaps the new intruders are beginning to sound like good news to them. These are on the fence, and the last thing they need is a judgmental put-down. Leave judgment to God. Let the church surround them with words and acts of love and mercy.

The second group is in greater spiritual danger. They no longer waver; their behavior makes it clear they have been lured away. They are "in the fire." Is it too late to restore them? This is no time to form a panel on post-baptismal sins and the fate of the lapsed. Let the church reaffirm its trust in the patience and the grace of God. Who is qualified to take the measure of God's love and name the persons who live beyond its reach? Let the church move close enough to "snatch them out of the fire." After all, who knows but what a portion of the reason these are now in spiritual danger lies in the apathy or indifference or insensitivity of the congregation at a critical time in the lives of these wandering souls. In any case, caring initiative and not blaming is the urgent need.

The third and final group seem to be the most deeply enmeshed in corrupt and unacceptable behavior. Even so, the instruction is to show mercy, "with fear." What fear? Most likely the fear of contamination, but the fear of falling into the same condition is not to paralyze the church. Remember Jesus and the leper. Jesus did not shout a blessing from a distance or over a wall; "Jesus stretched out his hand and touched him" (Mark 1:41). Neither can the church fully provide the good news of Christ by mailing checks to projects. It helps, of course, but relationships are both the means and the end of the Christian faith. The writer knows the dangers; that is the point of the precaution: "with fear."

The risks are basically two. The first we have already mentioned: the risk of succumbing to the same diseases. No one is so strong of spirit as to be able to be confident of never slipping. The overconfident tend to fall in rather than to lift out. The second risk is that of criticism from some of one's brothers and sisters. The scripture says that the way of the transgressor is hard, but so also is the way of the one who tries to help. To have one's actions and motives attacked, and by fellow believers, is indeed painful. So painful, in fact, as to reduce some to pools of pity, concerned but afraid to act. Some of the criticism arises because forgiveness appears to spectators as condoning. But still the church should not be surprised. Of the one whose mercy is our only hope, it was often said, "Look at him! He is eating with tax collectors and sinners."

CONCLUDING DOXOLOGY
Jude 24–25

24 **Now to him who is able to keep you from falling, and to make you stand without blemish in the presence of his glory with rejoicing,** 25 **to the only God our Savior, through Jesus Christ our Lord, be glory, majesty, power, and authority, before all time and now and forever. Amen.**

To those who attend worship services, this lofty and beautiful closing is likely the most familiar portion of Jude. Ministers quite frequently recite this doxology as a benediction, but it is not location in a service of worship that distinguishes a doxology from a benediction. A benediction (a word of God's favor on the listeners) may appear prior to the conclusion (for example, Rom. 15:13 and 33; 1 Thess. 3:13; and 2 Thess. 2:16–17 are benedictions well in advance of the letter's ending), just as a doxology (an expression of praise to God) may come at the end, as in Jude. Granted, the two forms may merge in function (as in Rom. 16:25–27), but the distinction is being made here because it is important to think about how Jude brings the letter to a close; that is, in a grand sweep of praise. Indictments of troublemakers and admonitions to the faithful are now over. After all, one cannot dwell on the difficulties forever. Those who try to make a career out of their problems soon wither from undernourishment and harden into knots of criticism. The frame for Christian living, for teaching and preaching, is worship. Jude knows that and lifts the congregation before the throne of God.

While the doxology in verses 24–25 could have been appropriately written to any church and can be appropriately recited over any gathering of worshipers, a closer look at its words and phrases reveal that it was addressed to this church in this circumstance. Notice: "able to keep you from falling." For a church unsettled and divided by intruders, the writer has repeatedly spoken of God's power to keep, to guard, to secure (vv. 1, 6, 13). Even so, the seductive influence of the intruders is sufficiently strong to make falling away a real danger (v. 21).

Notice: "to make you stand without blemish in the presence of his glory." Here the scene is the final judgment when all answer to God. This expression gathers up in a positive way all the references and allusions to the end time sprinkled throughout the letter (vv. 1, 6, 13, 14, 15, 18, 21). Notice: "before all time and now and forever." Some ascriptions of praise use space categories (the heavens, the earth, the subterranean regions in Phil. 2:10) to say that no reach of the universe is beyond the grace and power of God. Here the categories are temporal, to say that God precedes creation, is not subject to the turbulence of history, and remains God after the end of all things. In the language of Hebrews, "the same yesterday and today and forever" (13:8) and of Revelation, "who is and who was and who is to come" (1:4), such terms serve to assure the destabilized and anxious. And in the present case the phrase presents God as the very opposite of the disturbers who are as temporary as clouds carried along by the winds, as stars wandering off course (vv. 12–13). Notice: "God our Savior." Although the expression is a bit rare in the New Testament (used eight times), it is fully appropriate to the theocentric language of the letter and to the Jewish traditions that surface frequently. God acts in judgment and grace, such actions being "through Jesus Christ our Lord." Sometimes Christians become so preoccupied with talk about Jesus or about the Holy Spirit that they forget that the central subject of both Testaments is God.

As for the ascription to God of glory, majesty, power, and authority, Jude seems to have been influenced by liturgical practice that became formalized quite early in its language about God. For example, a very similar expression was added to the Matthean form of the Lord's Prayer (6:9–13) for use in the church's liturgy, and it became so firmly attached that it made its way into the King James Bible of 1611, and continues to be recited in most Protestant churches today: "For thine is the kingdom, and the power, and the glory forever." A likely source for the church's formula of praise was David's doxology before all the people in anticipation of Solomon's building the temple. David ascribed to God glory, majesty, power, and authority (1 Chron. 29:10–13).

We assume Jude's letter was read in the church assembled for worship.

We also assume the writer knew beforehand that the letter would be received in that setting and imagined its reception during the writing. All good letter writers attend not only to the sending but to the receiving, and picture the letter being read on a commuter train, at a lunch table, in an office, in a hospital bed, in a dorm room, or in a bedside chair. Such predictions are sometimes amiss, but they still influence both the message and the mood of a letter. Jude had the advantage of knowing the circumstance of the letter's reception. The church would be gathered for praise, prayer, alms, and perhaps a meal together during which concerns would be shared. With that in mind the author began, "May mercy, peace, and love be yours in abundance" and concluded with this doxology. Surely the reader did not say, "We interrupt this worship to hear a letter from Jude." The letter itself was an act of worship.

A FINAL WORD

Experiencing again the doxology in verses 24–25 prompts a reflection on the letter of Jude and in a sense on the letters of Peter as well. A generation ago it was fairly common to hear and read of New Testament letters that they were, with two or three exceptions, rather hastily dashed off to address crises and therefore were lacking in literary value. In addition, early Christians as a lot were viewed as unlettered peasants who could not be expected to do more than put the necessary sentences together. Such talk contributed to the popular portrait of the humble beginnings of the church, and the church enjoyed the portrait. After all, every institution, once it can afford the marble stairs and the golden candlestick recalls with pleasure the log cabin in its past. And, to be sure, there were log cabins, and poverty, and illiteracy among the followers of Jesus, and properly so. After all, "whosoever will may come."

But there were some members of those communities of faith who knew how to write and to write well. Recently to the study of the New Testament have been brought understandings of ancient rhetoric and letter writing, and no longer do the letter writers of the New Testament appear as literary pygmies. Granted, we do not know the names of the persons who actually penned many of the epistles, but whoever they were, they were members of the church with literary skills appropriate to the grand good news to be shared.

The text of Jude, for instance, and especially in its Greek form, reveals an author well read in a range of current literature and skilled in the use of repetition, quotations, passing allusions, refrains, irony, vivid images, and even caricatures. He knew how to move from negative to positive and to end with a flourish in the presence of God. All this without once allowing art to obscure the truth sought and shared. And the letter is not theologically deprived. To be sure, some favorite tenets of the faith are not voiced, perhaps sacrificed to brevity and to need. If that be conceded, then what is said of God, of Christ, and of the Holy Spirit should draw from the church a genuine Amen.

For Further Reading

1 Peter

Achtemeier, Paul. "First Peter." *Harper's Bible Commentary*. San Francisco: Harper & Row, 1988.

Beare, F. W. *The First Epistle of Peter*. 3d ed. Oxford: Blackwell, 1970.

Best, Ernest. *First Peter*. New Century Bible. Grand Rapids: Wm. B. Eerdmans Publishing Co., 1982.

Cranfield, C.E.B. *The First Epistle of Peter*. London: SCM, 1954.

Dalton, W. J., "The First Epistle of Peter." *The New Jerome Biblical Commentary*. Englewood Cliffs, N.J.: Prentice-Hall, 1990.

Elliott, J. H. *A Home for the Homeless*. Philadelphia: Fortress Press, 1981.

Johnson, Luke T. *The Writings of the New Testament*. Philadelphia: Fortress Press, 1986. 430–41.

Kelly, J.N.D. *A Commentary on the Epistles of Peter and Jude*. New York: Harper & Row, 1969.

Perkins, Pheme. *First and Second Peter, James, and Jude*. Interpretation. Louisville, Ky.: John Knox Press, 1995.

2 Peter

Bauckham, Richard. *Jude, 2 Peter*. Waco, Tex.: Word, 1983.

———. "Second Peter." *Harper's Bible Commentary*. San Francisco: Harper & Row, 1988.

Johnson, Luke T. *The Writings of the New Testament*. Philadelphia: Fortress Press, 1986. 442–52.

Kelly, J.N.D. *A Commentary on the Epistles of Peter and Jude*. New York: Harper & Row, 1969.

Neyrey, Jerome H. "The Second Epistle of Peter." *The New Jerome Biblical Commentary*. Englewood Cliffs, N.J.: Prentice-Hall, 1990.

Pearson, Birger. "James, 1–2 Peter, Jude." In *The New Testament and Its*

Modern Interpreters. E. Epp and M. MacRae, eds. Philadelphia: Fortress Press, 1989.

Perkins, Pheme. *First and Second Peter, James, and Jude.* Interpretation. Louisville, Ky.: John Knox Press, 1995.

Sidebottom, E. M. *James, Jude, 2 Peter.* Grand Rapids: Wm. B. Eerdmans Publishing Co., 1982.

Jude

Bauckham, Richard. *Jude, 2 Peter.* Waco, Tex.: Word, 1983.

———. "Jude." *Harper's Bible Commentary.* San Francisco: Harper & Row, 1988.

Johnson, Luke T. *The Writings of the New Testament.* Philadelphia: Fortress Press, 1986.

Kelly, J.N.D. *A Commentary on the Epistles of Peter and Jude.* New York: Harper & Row, 1969.

Neyrey, Jerome H. "The Epistle of Jude." *The New Jerome Biblical Commentary.* Englewood Cliffs, N.J.: Prentice-Hall, 1990.

Pearson, Birger. "James, 1–2 Peter, Jude." In *The New Testament and Its Modern Interpreters.* E. Epp and G. MacRae, eds. Philadelphia: Fortress Press, 1989.

Perkins, Pheme. *First and Second Peter, James, and Jude.* Interpretation. Louisville, Ky.: John Knox Press, 1995.

Sidebottom, E. M. *James, Jude, 2 Peter.* Grand Rapids: Wm. B. Eerdmans Publishing Co., 1982.

Note: The *Revised English Bible* (Oxford University Press and Cambridge University Press, 1989) is abbreviated REB.